PRAISE FOR FREE TO PARENT

"A few years ago when I was writing my book "21 Ways to Connect with Your Kids", Ellen Schuknecht submitted a story about bullying and how to help your kids respond that really resonated with both me and my readers. Since then, I've known that if I need good, solid, Christian parenting advice for kids of any age, Ellen Schuknecht is a go-to resource. "Free to Parent" is full of Ellen's wisdom in addition to her daughter Erin's in-the-trenches stories and advice. As I read, I saw the joy that can come when parents free themselves from common discipline traps and look instead for the hope, peace and love that can only come from Christ. Woven with real-life stories and heart-touching ideas, is a perfect step to help you find joy in parenting and raise kids that truly love Jesus. I highly recommend this book for parents at any stage."

-- Kathi Lipp, author of more than 10 books, including "21 Ways to Connect with Your Kids" and "I Need Some Help Here! Hope for When Your Kids Don't Go According to Plan"

"Ellen and Erin inspire readers to rise above the mundane, rules-driven parenting advice of our day. In its place, they empower parents to reach out to God to find a joy-filled way to parent. Not only will parents become deeply connected to the God of love and to their children, but their wise advice will also help parents nurture and grow ⸱⸱⸱⸱⸱⸱ who desire to become Christ-followers, God-seekers, an⸱ ⸱⸱⸱⸱⸱⸱⸱ that make a difference in this world."

—Susan G Ma⸱⸱⸱⸱⸱⸱⸱⸱ ⸱⸱ge Adventure and *Countdow⸱*

Free to Parent

ESCAPE PARENTING TRAPS AND LIBERATE YOUR CHILD'S SPIRIT

Ellen M Schuknecht
with
Erin M MacPherson

Family Wings, LLC
www.familywings.org
Austin, TX

© 2014 by Ellen M Schuknecht and Erin M MacPherson, second printing

Published by Family Wings, LLC
www.familywings.org
Austin, TX 78652

Printed in the United States of America

Library of Congress Cataloging-in-Publication Data is on file at the Library of Congress, Washington, DC.

ISBN: 069223120X
ISBN: 978-0692231203

Unless otherwise indicated, Scripture quotations are from the Holy Bible, English Standard Version, copyright ©2011 by Crossway Bibles.

To protect the privacy of those who have shared their stories with the authors, some details and names have been changed.

ES: To my precious grandchildren:

Josiah, Kate, Jude, Hadassah, Greta, William, Asa, Elsie, Alma and Baby E who waits for us in Ethiopia

EM: To my wonderful mommy friends who lift me up and make me a better mom.

CONTENTS

ACKNOWLEDGEMENTS

Writing a book as a mother-daughter team has been a delightful journey, uniting not only our hearts around this project but also weaving together stories from both of our generations.

We would like to thank the following people for their insights, support, and encouragement without which this book would not have been written:

To our husbands who have lovingly supported this project and cheered us on.

To Troy & Stevi Schuknecht and Peter & Alisa Dusan who listen to our ideas, gave sound feedback and encouraged us to keep writing.

To our kids: Joey, Kate, Jude, Hadassah, Greta, William, Asa, Elsie and Alma who provide ample stories to write about.

To Susan Mathis whose expertise in editing and content greatly enhanced this book.

To Rachelle Garnder who listened to our idea and gave us the courage to put them onto paper.

To Kathi Lipp who fielded our questions and helped us set direction.

To Jef Fowler who has encouraged us and gave permission to include "The Veritas Valiant" in this book, something he created.

And to our many friends who shared stories and suggestions, providing depth and insight to this book.

We are deeply grateful for each one of you who have inspired us and made this book possible.

INTRODUCTION

(Erin)

Have you ever wondered if the "parenting experts" got it wrong? That, just maybe, the tried-and-true tricks and tips on Christian parenting are actually hurting our kids' faith rather than building their faith?

We know that's a big leap—and we know many of you may be tempted to toss this book aside and pick up something less...provocative. But bear with us.

We're not writing this to confuse you or to tell you to change who you are or what you do. We're writing this book to free you. To give you hope. And to show you that there is a loving, fresh, kind, hopeful, and—dare we say it?—joyful way to parent our kids.

A few weeks ago, my eight-year-old son Joey came home from soccer practice in a terrible mood. He flung off his cleats and ripped off his shin guards. Then he sulked his way into the kitchen and tossed his water bottle into the sink. He turned to me with a snarl and said, "I want an ice cream bar!"

I whipped around, my mind flooding with all of the disciplinary truths that have been engrained in me since I became a parent.

Kids must show respect, or they will lose all privileges.

If an adult says something, a kid should do it.

Never give in to a kid who is throwing a tantrum.

I growled back, "Why would I give you what you want when you're being rude? Go upstairs and take a shower, and then come down when you have a better attitude!"

There. That would solve that. Good parenting 101.

Joey started to turn toward the stairs, but then I saw his eyes widen. He turned back, his jaw set. "You can't make me."

I can't make him? Sure I can!

More of those "good Christian mom" phrases flooded my mind.

First-time obedience.

Consistent consequences.

Nip the cycle of disrespect in the bud.

"Fine," I quipped. "But if you're not in the shower in the next two minutes, you're losing all screen time for a week!" I bit my lip to keep from smiling. *That* would teach him not to talk back to me.

Joey's shoulder's fell. He turned and trudged up the stairs, banging his fist into the wall with each step. I heard the shower turn on, I heard the towel cabinet open, and I heard my son's door slam. And I smiled.

He had done what I had asked him to.

His will had been broken.

I had won.

A few hours later, I was tucking my other son into bed, and Joey came and stood by the door and leaned against the door jam.

"I... I... uh..." he mumbled. I turned to him and saw a look in his eye that made me pause.

Was he holding back tears?

Was my son—the kid who took pride in the fact that he was strong and tough and hadn't even cried when he had fallen off of his bike and dislocated his jaw—about to cry?

I frowned. It was bedtime (and we all know that kids need consistency with sleeping and eating schedules, right?). And besides, Joey *had* demonstrated a terrible attitude earlier. Moreover, I needed to get the kids to bed on time so I could pack for an upcoming trip. I simply didn't have time for his...shenanigans.

Was he trying to manipulate me? Was he trying to score an overtime point after I had so clearly won the battle earlier?

My mind echoed with the many tricks and tips yet again.

Don't let kids manipulate you.

Stay consistent.

But...one look at those weepy green eyes and my heart clenched. Empathy flooded my soul.

My son was hurting, and I didn't know why.

Motherly instinct took over, and I pushed aside the things I'd learned in the parenting books. I grabbed my son and made him some hot chocolate, and then we sat on the couch together. Finally I asked, "What's up?"

"Nothing. I just wanted to talk to you." Joey sighed, and his eyes slowly drifted toward the door.

Something *was* up, so I pulled my big boy onto my lap and asked again. "No, really? What's wrong?"

A lone tear trickled down his cheek.

"I'm scared mom!" my brave boy admitted. "At practice my friend told me that yesterday there was a plane that crashed into the ocean, and, well, I know you are going on a plane this week. What if your plane crashes?"

My Joey started to sob, his shoulders shaking, his breath coming in groans.

And my heart broke.

Joey had come home from practice terrified that he was going to lose *me*, overcome by overwhelming fear. And I had parented him into a hard, cold corner. I had pushed his emotions and feelings aside and forced him to do what was "right" without stopping to think about his heart.

About his soul.

About my precious boy—who was scared and alone - needed his mom's love and care, not just discipline.

How often do we as parents do that? With the best intentions, we follow all the rules, doing our best to "expect obedience" without ever truly seeing them for who they are: broken, flawed, emotional, and struggling people who God wants to use for His big purposes. If only we let Him.

Before we go any further, we need to make one thing clear. We are *not* telling you that things like discipline and obedience should be tossed aside. Far from it! We are simply suggesting that if we don't have an emotional connection with our kids, then all the consequences we dole out, all the lectures we speak, and all the parenting truths we instill in them will fall on deaf hearts.

Not deaf ears, mind you—for we have little doubt that most Christian kids "know" right from wrong at an early age. These kids have heard it all, and they know what is good and beautiful and what is downright ugly. But do these kids truly desire to do right, while rejecting wrong, in their hearts? That takes a lot more work.

And that's what this book is about.

Not discipline.

Not obedience.

Not hammering concepts like respect and honesty and hard work and responsibility into our kids' heads.

This book is about gently and lovingly guiding eternity into their hearts.

Chapter 1

REPLACE YOU WITH HIM

(Ellen)

I started writing this book more than 40 years ago.

I had a messy childhood, and though it wasn't necessarily "bad," I sure didn't grow up in a Christian home. My parents were ethical and moral and kind and hardworking, but neither of them knew Jesus. And it showed in the way my siblings and I were raised.

I remember a time when I was about eight years old, and I tried to bake a cake for my sister's birthday. My parents were both very busy people, so they rarely (if ever) helped us do things. I never remember either of my parents helping me with my homework or coming to a school event. And so I knew that if I wanted to bake a cake, I was on my own.

I thought I could do it, so I carefully read the recipe and measured the ingredients and popped the cake batter into the oven. I watched the timer meticulously, imagining a beautiful tower of pink and white cake, a perfect and heartfelt gift for my family.

Unfortunately, it flopped. Badly. I don't know if I forgot to put the eggs in or if the recipe simply didn't work. But my beautiful cake was a crumbled, gooey mess.

My two sisters walked in and saw my disaster, and they started laughing. They called it "Ellen's Cherry Flop."

I was devastated.

I so wished that someone, anyone, would have noticed my effort. That someone would have seen how hard I had tried, would have understood that my heart had been in the right place as I had carefully mixed and baked. But no one saw *that*. They just saw my mess.

And as I looked at my family—from my mom who had ignored the disaster entirely except to tell my sisters and me to "work it out"—to my sisters who were sing-songing the words, "cherry flo-op, cherry flo-op"—I started to cry.

And then I ran away.

I grabbed my jacket and took off running across the acres-wide cow pastures that surrounded our house and hid in a small meadow next to the creek. I sat there, feeling completely misunderstood and uncared for, and I wished that someone cared enough to come find me. To tell me it was okay. To let me know that I was loved and cherished and that my mistakes didn't define me.

But no one came.

And so I sat there, for what seemed like hours, rehashing the morning and muddling over my good intentions, my failed result, and the fact that no one came to my rescue. No one threw me a lifeline. No one saw my heart.

I went home that day to an unsafe house. Not physically unsafe (my parents never abused us) but an emotionally unsafe home. I had nowhere to turn with my emotional messes. I had no one to trust. I had no one to disciple me to a better way.

Family life was messy—and my siblings responded to the pain and isolation with rebellion. By the time they were young adults, our family had a plethora of issues ranging from teen pregnancy to drugs and alcohol to involvement in cults. It was scary. And we desperately needed something more.

I responded differently than my siblings. Since I am a people pleaser by nature and had accepted Jesus in Sunday School, something in my heart told me there was a better way. And so I did everything I could to grow and learn so that I would one day be able to escape the mess of my childhood. I wanted to live in a way that was productive and that would lead to life. I innately knew I was made for something more.

After I left home for college, that mustard seed of faith began to grow. Through several caring professors, loving Christian friends, and a new church body, I began to learn what faith really meant. I began to study my Bible, to pray, to journal, and to grow. When I started dating my future husband, Glen, as a senior in college, I longed for security and spiritual connection. I saw this possibility in Glen, who was rooted in his faith. He had grown up in a Christian home and he understood what faith truly meant.

I saw in him what I had never known in my own family: faith, truth, hope, connectedness...Jesus.

We got married. And that was when I started writing this book.

In my desire to escape the pain and isolation of my childhood, I had vowed that my own kids would grow up in a home that nurtured their faith, a home where they learned to truly love and follow Christ. They would live in a home where their hearts learned to see Jesus.

I wanted this—desperately—but I had no idea how to give it to them. Yet, I was not going to let that stop me. Armed with my Early Childhood Education degree and a steely determination to break the cycles that had plagued my childhood, I started to read books. To pray. To talk to experts. To do my best to figure out how I could raise my kids in a way that honored Jesus, and in doing so, teach them to truly see and follow Him.

I read all the right books and memorized all the right strategies, and—don't laugh—started to analyze the families I saw in our community. The child who threw a tantrum in the restaurant? I watched him from a distance and took mental notes about how his parents should have handled the situation. And the family at church who arrived frantic and late and with two crying kids? Well, I knew how to solve that. I had figured it out! I had cracked the code to parenting. I knew what all of the big wigs said, and I knew just how to apply it.

I was going to be super mom.

I remember sitting in our tiny first home and jotting down all of the "rules" to being a good parent. A checklist of sorts. If my kid starts to throw a tantrum, Dr. So-and-So says to do this, and if my kid is disobedient, well, then obviously I should do that.

Then I got pregnant. I was thrilled. I could finally put all my parenting expertise to use and have living proof that it works. This book was going to be a "slam dunk"—and parents would come from far and wide to see that, yes, if you just applied consistent consequences and expected first-time obedience, then naturally your kid would be perfectly behaved at all times.

I'm sure you can imagine how that worked out for me.

My oldest daughter, Erin, was born. And from day one, she did not fit the mold of any book I had read. She was emotional and determined, passionate and creative, feisty and...yes, disobedient. She threw food at walls and threw tantrums in stores, and did all the things I swore my kids would never do. And my little bag of tricks—you know, the bag that would definitely work because the experts said it would—failed me again and again.

I quickly learned that all the foolproof ideas spelled out in books and the brilliant ideas I had formulated on paper were really not very foolproof at all. Not only did my daughter fail to respond to everything I thought I knew, but also as our family grew, each of my three kids responded differently than my firstborn did. I couldn't figure it out.

Familiar feelings returned. I felt alone, desperate, and like I was failing at the one thing I wanted most for my kids. And I set my book aside for years!

Instead, I focused on my kids—those three desperately messy (but completely loved!) children that God had blessed me with. It was at that point, I realized God first needed to orchestrate a series of experiences that would not only establish my own inheritance in Christ, but also develop within me an understanding of what it looked like for parents to raise kids who would remain rooted in their faith.

The book I started writing so many years ago would have been tinged with desperation. With hopelessness. With ideas and tips and suggestions that may have seemed good on paper, but that never got to the heart of the issue: Our kids need Jesus. And they need parents who are willing to wholeheartedly follow Him as they guide their children toward Him.

Now, forty years after I began this journey to writing—and living—this book, I feel like I've come full circle. My three kids are in their thirties and raising kids of their own. My nine grandchildren now struggle in the same manner my own kids struggled, and I am able to help my kids work through the same issues I struggled with as a parent. I have spent my career leading schools, supporting kids, counseling and educating families.

And like forty long years ago, my heart continues to beat for families, especially as it relates to developing a spiritual heritage that can be passed on to the next generation and then on to the next. But now, God has given me something new: A sense of hope, a sense of clarity, a sense of vision for what parenting can mean. And what our kids can become.

This book, the one I've picked up and started writing again after forty years of collecting dust, is not just a collection of key principles that I consider most important in raising kids who remain devoted to Jesus. This book also reflects my own life story—a story that's messy and real and not perfect. It's a story that God is still working on just like I pray He is doing with your kids.

Getting back to Jesus in our parenting

Imagine you're about to start a hike through a vast and flowered meadow. Distracted by the giant snowy mountains that stretch out in the distance, you take your first step, just to the left and a little off the path you had intended. Just one step. Just a tiny bit off. At first, you are only inches from where you were supposed to be. The view is the same. The flowers still bloom blue and fragrant. Everything seems to be virtually the same.

But then you take another step. And another. And before long the mountains loom to your right instead of straight ahead, the scenery starts to change, and the path begins to become quite rugged. After several miles down the new path you took, that one small misstep—just a few inches in the wrong direction—has led you miles off your intended path, and in the wrong direction from where you wanted to go!

This is what I believe has happened to many Christian parents.

They set off on the journey of parenting and it's undeniably beautiful, an incredible gift from God. They wanted to walk the right path, to do it right, to raise kids who would develop a sense of genuine faith that would lead them to love Jesus wholeheartedly and love people mercifully. But in their quest to do it right, they started to follow a set of subscribed rules, rules that replaced love and connection with obedience and discipline and control. Just one little step in the wrong direction.

And that step took them miles off the path.

This is what happened to my friend Sarah. She and her now deceased husband had done their best to "do it right" with their three kids—following the advice of Christian experts—as they maintained obedience and godliness in their home. That included a strong hand and a heaping dose of tough love. They had faithfully attended church and home schooled all three kids. But more than that, they subscribed to the notion that first-time obedience and consistent discipline *were* the key to raising godly kids. And so they pressed their kids to obey and be respectful, and they consistently punished their children's wrongdoing.

As a mom, Sarah says she began to grow anxious each time they committed a mistake or behaved inappropriately, and she agonized over what she might have done wrong to cause the grievance. Surely, she concluded, if her parenting was above reproach, her kids would follow suit.

She desired a loving relationship with them—but not at the cost of them straying from the expectations she had placed on them. She could not be their friend. She was their mother, and as such she had the job of making sure they turned out as she envisioned, as the experts had taught her.

Does this sound familiar?

Sadly, the end of the story may sound familiar as well. When Sarah's three, seemingly obedient kids left home for college, they also left behind any desire for a relationship with their parents along with the God they proclaimed to serve. They walked out of a tightly controlled nest and joined arms with the "outsiders" who did not seem to be nearly as "evil" as their parents had judged them to be. In fact, some were far easier to connect with than their own parents were. All three discovered compassion, acceptance, and genuine connection outside their own home and outside the church. The three are now in their 20's, and none have returned to their home or their parents' hearts.

Her story represents so many similar stories I hear day after day. Anxious and fearful parents do everything they know to do to make sure their kids learn right from wrong. And in the process, these fearful parents raise their kids in an environment that misses the true point of Christian parenting—nurturing their souls. They create an environment that—yes, I'm going to say it—has *caused* countless kids to adopt a shallow faith. One that is solely aimed at avoiding punishment instead of embracing a genuine faith that truly desires God.

As parents, we simply have to stop doing what hasn't worked for far too long! It's time to turn from the prevailing dogma about parenting through discipline and control. We must move back to the basics, to the place where we as parents lead our children as our Heavenly Father leads us.

It's time for us to hike backward for a bit, to return to that moment where we first took that tiny step in the wrong direction, and to refocus our eyes on the looming mountains ahead. We must focus our eyes on Jesus and not the dogmas of pop parenting psychology. It's time to replace our own rules, ideas, thoughts and hopes with Jesus. Simply Jesus.

And with that, it's time for us to prioritize connection more than control, faith more than fear, discipleship more than discipline. It's time for us to treat our kids the way Jesus treats us—with a heaping dose of grace, mercy, and love.

Now, before you toss this book into the trash can and label me as a heretic, please understand that I am a devoted follower of Jesus and I stand on the inerrancy of the Bible. I desire deeply to see that each of your children comes to know and love the Lord with all his or her heart, soul, and might. I love God's Word, His Truth. I stand firmly on the Rock.

But I believe many of us have fallen victim to leaving the path of parenting God speaks of in His Word and straying from the plan that He lovingly beckons us to follow. For too long, the idea that parenting largely means inflicting strict control and forced obedience on our children has flourished in the Christian church. I want to see this change so that the very heart of parenting will start to reflect the highest and deepest virtues of our Christian faith.

That's why I couldn't write this book so many years ago. I had also stepped off the God-given path, and walked toward the psychologically prescribed hills of man's making, instead of keeping my eyes on the God-created mountains of parenting promises. I thought I knew truth, but instead, I only knew rules. I knew human formulas that were aimed at controlling and demanding obedience, but I had no idea how to connect with my kids at the heart level. Like Jesus does with me.

I'm still learning what this truly means and looks like, but I can say that I've hiked several miles, back to the start, back to the place where the path divided. I've refocused my eyes on what really matters. And I firmly believe that the highest and the deepest core aim of parenting must first be about connection to our children's spirits and not simply about their obedience or their compliance to rules. While obedience and compliance are still important, if we only focus on making our children behave, we will miss the true heart of parenting.

When obedience and compliance are the most important aims, parents tend to rely on punishment, threats, and bribes. This fosters an atmosphere of excessive control and management. Parents may get obedience as an outcome, but often it is performance-driven compliance resulting from concern about getting into trouble, fear of rejection, or merely as a means of getting what kids want. Obedience may appear to be good on the outside, but the heart often remains distant and untouched. Only a true heart change will hold up over time.

Yet when a connected relationship is the highest and deepest aim, grace-based practices are put into place. These are parenting practices that are discipleship driven rather than punishment driven, and they are ones that result in reachable-thus-teachable hearts. More than performance-driven critics, we as parents need to become trusted, loving advisors—where our children find connection and acceptance regardless of what is taking place in their lives. When a loving relationship is the aim, it is dramatically more likely that sincere obedience will form in the hearts and minds of our children. Without a connected, loving relationship, our influence is minimal at best.

Really, it's no different with God. We love Him *because* He first loved us—right in the middle of our mess. Our trust and security must be rooted, not in our performance for Him, but in what He accomplished for us on the cross. His connected relationship with us creates a reachable-thus-teachable heart in us so that we *want* to obey Him.

I asked my sweet friend Sarah—the one from the beginning of this chapter—what she would do differently if she could go back and raise her three children again. She took no time in stating, *"I would emphasize the grace and love of God more than do's and don'ts; I would trust the Holy Spirit and not my own efforts; I would manage less and let them fail more so that they would grow responsible; and I would be more loving and less judgmental."*

What a powerful confession!

Thankfully, Sarah believes God is not done with her family yet. As a widowed grandmother, she now makes it her aim to form a loving connection with her children and grandchildren. And this brings her joy instead of anxiety and hope instead of fear. Her story is for parents or grandparents at any age, because it is never too late for any of us to form loving connections with our kids and grandkids.

Are you ready to do things differently and to see how Jesus treats us so we can learn how to treat our kids the same way? Mercifully, justly, hopefully, fearlessly—and lovingly?

I know that I am. And I hope this book can be a start.

A prayer for surrender

Father God, I desire to trust you with all my heart rather than lean on my own understanding. Cast out fear and bring peace to my troubled heart. I desire to place my trust in who You declare Yourself to be and not in who I am. Teach me to acknowledge you in every aspect of my parenting and set a straight path before my family and me. I am grateful to be saved by faith and not by my own doing, which fails me time and time again. Teach me to model surrender to my children. I desire to steadfastly abide in you, my Rock and my Redeemer, and to lead my children in doing the same. Amen

Verses for further study

Proverbs 3:5-6
Ephesians 2:8-9
Philippians 4:13
John 15:1-27

Chapter 2

REPLACE OBEDIENCE WITH DESIRE

(Ellen and Erin)

Whoa! Wait a second!

We can imagine your mind is already reeling just reading the title of this chapter—your heartbeat has probably sped up, and you may be crafting an indignant email to us explaining why obedience is the cornerstone of disciplined parenting and, well, if our kids don't learn to obey us, how are they going to learn to obey teachers and bosses and... the law?

We get it. Obedience *is* important—and without it we'd have a troop of unruly two-year-olds ruling our worlds, demanding goldfish crackers at naptime, informing us that they don't have to eat their peas if they don't want to and there is nothing that mommy can do about it. We're not saying it's not important that our kids obey, but we are simply suggesting that we need to rethink our definition—and philosophy—of obedience.

If our kids only obey us in order to avoid a consequence, then are they really obeying? Or are they just acting like rats in a cage, pressing a button to get a desired reward? We think it's the latter, and if that's true, then shouldn't we reassess the way we raise our kids? Do we want them to form a genuine, connected obedience based on their faith, or do we want them to simply obey?

Aristotle stated that, "the aim of education is to make the pupil like and dislike what he ought." He was right! As we raise our kids, our aim should be more about helping our kids to desire what is good than about simply teaching them what is good.

Do we want our kids to simply know right from wrong? To understand a list of rules they need to obey in order to get what they want? Or is our aim deeper and richer—that they would grow to "love the Lord their God with all their heart and with all their soul and with all their might" (Deuteronomy 6:5)?

The truth is, it's not enough to simply teach our kids to obey. When our end goal is to help our kids truly desire God, concepts like "first-time obedience" and even "consistent consequences" start to fall flat. These concepts—while useful as parenting tools—can teach our kids to have head knowledge of what is right and what is wrong. But going far beyond that, our kids need to learn how to direct the desires of their heart on a foundation of connected faith so they will understand how to truly desire what is good and right and beautiful and then reject what is evil.

Acceptable performance with cold hearts

There's no greater peril to authentic faith than allowing your child's walk with God to become merely outward obedience. I would prefer to see kids blatantly and openly disobey than to pretend they are obedient while inwardly remaining unrepentant. Why is it so easy for parents to fall into this trap? I believe most wind up in this snare with good intentions. We desire to be good parents and then naturally look for external evidence as validation. And we want to please others. Furthermore, we fear being judged by others for the behaviors of our children. Charming Kate, who knows how to perform especially when adults are watching, provides her parents with a "pat on the back" but Wild William causes the wind to go out of their sails. When we assume that going through the motions indicates an authentic heart, we may fail to examine what is really going on.

It's easy to be deceived by well-behaved kids, who have learned how to look clean on the outside but still remain dirty on the inside. They then grow up into young adults who are accustomed to pretending and see no need for internal transformation. They get along just fine, getting what they want without all the pain of examining their own hearts. And that's exactly what we promote when outward obedience is the highest aim within the Christian family; individuals who can serve God in outward ways, yet bluntly disobey Him by failing to deal with anger, greed, lust, pride, and bitterness in their hearts.

We all know the tragic stories of men and women who seemed so devoted to serving God, who wind up hurting so many when the true condition of their hearts eventually surfaces: the youth pastor caught up in pornography, the deacon involved in a five-year affair, the school teacher secretly pursuing one of his students, the CEO of a ministry caught embezzling funds. These are people who have attempted to hide their real intentions under a disguise of performance. They have learned to express false integrity for personal gain while maintaining distant hearts from the Lord.

That's why we discourage parents from forcing kids to express sorrow before they are sincerely sorry. Your child may simply be learning how to act on the outside in order to avoid consequences. Begin as early as you can to foster an authentic faith, which is an "inside out" experience. Do this by encouraging honest expressions of what is really going on in the heart. Desire authenticity over pretense; openness over secrecy; and honest conversation over what you wish to hear. Be a loving, safe person with whom your kids can share what is really going on in their hearts. Sometimes all that is needed for a heart to repent is the opportunity to safely express the truth.

The mind informs, but the heart motivates

(Erin)

I can guarantee you that my son Joey knows that teasing and taunting his little sister is wrong. In fact, he's done his fair share of extra chores and time-outs as he's learned that pestering her until she cries isn't the right or kind way to treat her.

Yet, shockingly, Joey still taunts and teases his sister to the point of tears on a regular basis. Why? Because it's fun to get a rise out of her. And the truth is, the fun of seeing his sister squirm is worth the consequence he knows will come.

Kids start learning right from wrong at an early age. Your average toddler probably knows that pitching herself onto the floor and kicking and screaming is wrong, but that doesn't stop her from getting a rise out of Mom by screaming in the toy aisle at Target. This isn't a reflection of the kid—or even on her desire to obey, but it is simply a reflection of the primary desire in the child's heart at that moment. She may want to obey, but if controlling Mom is something she wants more, then she will do what it takes to usurp Mom's control. Think about these examples:

- A four-year-old knows that taking a toy from a friend is wrong, but if she wants the toy badly enough, she will still take it.
- An eight-year-old knows that telling a lie is wrong, but if keeping out of trouble matters more, he will lie to get out of trouble.
- A fourteen-year-old knows that gossip is ugly, but if being the deliverer of juicy information matters more, she will gossip.
- A sixteen-year-old knows that cheating is wrong, but if getting a good grade is more important than honesty, he will cheat.

Each of these kids knows *what* the right thing to do is. But they don't *want* to do it. And unless a child has grown to rightly order their desires, their selfish human nature will kick in. It's simply not enough to know the difference between what is good and what is bad. Kids also need to learn to love one and hate the other deep in their heart.

Desire impacts our decisions

(Ellen)

I had sat through a seven-hour (yes, seven-hour!) meeting with our school board during which we had addressed issues facing the school. Earlier in the day, I had listened to complaints in which several families declared their intention to leave our school (based on gossip instead of truth). I felt like I was on the edge of a meltdown. A good, old-fashioned meltdown—complete with crying, whining, and binge eating dark chocolate.

Each disgruntled family felt like a nail piercing my heart because I took each one as a personal failure—as if my actions and decisions had disappointed them. As I drove home that night, I was committed to resigning the next day, because this was not what I had signed up for.

Here I was again, working overtime to please others. I cried out to God: *"Why do I try so hard to meet people's expectations—only to find that I always fall short?"* I wanted nothing more than to jump ship that night. The demands of developing and running a start-up school bombarded me constantly and they came from all directions—students, teachers, parents, and the board. Any decision I made or any action I took seemed to leave someone unhappy. Not a pleasant place for an unwavering people-pleaser to be.

That night as I prayed, echoes of discontent ran through my head. Winning the approval of others mattered more to me than anything, and it was clearly impossible to please everyone—or anyone, it seemed. So, I wanted out! Desperately.

I woke Glen at 1 A.M. to tell him, "I quit, and you can't make me change my mind!" With that I rolled into bed, turning my back to my husband, whom I assumed would be disappointed with me for being unable to keep all the families and staff—and myself—happy all the time. But he wasn't disappointed in me. Instead, Glen sat up and began to ask me a few questions. Why did I want to quit when only weeks before I had deeply wanted to be an integral part of developing the school? Why did my desires seem to change so drastically—and so quickly? After hours of prayer and conversation, we came to the conclusion that it had everything to do with that deep, deep desire of my heart. And at that point in my life, my desire to please others trumped everything else.

I finally came to the place where I was able to ask the Lord to remove me from my job *only* if it was His will. If He wanted me to stay, however, I begged Him to change the deepest desires of my heart and create in me a renewed desire to please Him with my work, above all else, instead of needing to please parents, students, teachers, and myself more.

That morning I began to find an amazing delight in the realization that, for the first time in a long time, I authentically desired to hear God's voice above all else—no matter what He would say. It dawned on me that it was Him alone that I needed to truly please, yet I did not have to earn His approval. With tears dripping down my face, I felt wholly approved of—and it was not dependent on my actions or the decision I might make. I could quit or I could stay, and God would still approve of me. It was an amazing revelation, and it changed my entire perspective.

I began to free myself from my people-pleasing ways that year. The temptation still exists, but I have learned how to cut it off. I can now see I had made many decisions in the past that were efforts to win approval. This pervasive need is waning, and although I still want to make people happy, it doesn't control my heart anymore. Jesus does. His desires are becoming my desires! And when anxiety begins to crowd Him out, I re-center myself through prayer and reflection. And little by little, He changes my desires.

I am still at Veritas Academy. These past ten years have been full of joy and blessing but have also included deep trials and tough attacks. I have displeased people many times by making decisions that did not meet with everyone's approval. But it matters less. God has rearranged what matters most in my heart. I delight myself in Him, and He, in turn, is giving me the desire of my heart. If I would have followed through with what my heart desired after that board meeting, I would have avoided some major struggles. But I also would have missed out on some of the grandest blessings God had in store for me. And at the top of the list is having my own grandchildren become students at my school!

My point in all this? We all make decisions in life based on what matters most to us—and so do our kids. So when our two-year-old is choosing to throw tantrums, or our seven-year-old is choosing to speak disrespectfully, we can't simply assume that a consistent consequence will change the desires of his heart. It may change the behavior, but as parents, we should want more—we should want our kids to know Jesus and follow His desires.

When a child's desires are rightly ordered, then he will deeply desire characteristics like self-control and godliness and kindness and patience—not because he will get in trouble if he doesn't display the fruit of the Spirit, but because he wants to please Jesus. Truth and a connected spiritual life become a part of who that child is! And when his heart is set on godly aims, he will make decisions and act in ways that supports those aims—and our hearts as parents will grow full of joy.

This character of heart—or lack thereof—affects kids at all ages, and in so many areas. If a two-year-old desires to play with toys rather than to stay in bed, you'd better believe he is going to spend half of the night out of his bed. And if an eight-year-old desires free time rather than academic success, she will most likely rush through her work so she can finish and go play outside. And if being accepted and approved by peers matters more than seeking to honor God by one's choices, a teenager can get caught up in sexual activity in an attempt to gain approval and acceptance. The same is true for alcohol and drugs. Teens know they are harmful. But *what matters the most* to them personally will ultimately drive their decisions. A longing for what is forbidden will only be consumed by a greater yearning for what God desires. That's why training our children to have God's desires is so important—even beginning in the earliest years.

Each of our children is created in the image of God and called to reflect Him in a manner that is unique to each of them. But the world so often gets in the way and entices them to focus on self-centered aims and foolish pursuits—an easier path for sure. That's why parents and teachers must be about the business of nourishing the minds and hearts of our children with God's higher goals by giving them regular diets of all that is true, good, and beautiful.

We need to set a higher standard for our children, one that is more appealing than the "path of least resistance." When they come to see God for who He is—a good, loving, kind Father who delights in them and desires good for them—then they will become motivated to love Him back and honor Him with their lives and choices. They will then grow to love what He loves, and they will be moved to do what is right and to reject what He hates.

Desire impacts our habits

Think about something you want really badly. Maybe it's to run a marathon. Or to lose twenty pounds. Or to get a job you really want. Or a house. Whatever it is, I'm guessing that you have developed a series of habits that will help you to reach that desire.

If you want to lose weight, you probably are trying to eat healthy and exercise more. If you want to buy a house, you are probably working hard to budget and keep track of your money. It's no different with character. If Johnny gets by with cheating, he begins to like the deceptiveness of it more and more. If Susie prefers being idle rather than being productive, lazy habits will begin to take hold.

Although this is a pretty simple concept, people often fail to translate it into their spiritual lives. Just as your worldly desires drive the formation of the lifestyle habits you live by, your spiritual desires are what will drive your spiritual habits, and ultimately, many of your life habits as well.

This concept relates to so many areas of our spiritual lives. If we truly desire God, we will desire to spend time with Him. We may take up a habit of praying continuously or spending time reading the Bible every day. Likewise, if we desire to please God, we will form habits that please Him—habits that reject dishonesty or impatience or anger or lust or whatever we struggle with.

TOOLS TO HELP KIDS DESIRE RIGHT

(Ellen)

Most Christian parents tend to have an easy time seeing that desire trumps simple obedience. But, if we're being honest, it's hard to teach our kids to actually desire what is right. Teaching obedience is easier (okay, sort of easier)—we can threaten and bribe and make kids fear doing wrong. We can show them a consistent set of consequences for their behavior. But teaching kids to earnestly desire God's ways beyond their selfish desires? That's just plain complicated—and takes lots and lots of hard work, prayer, and a great big heaping measure of faith.

There is no magic formula—no simple 1-2-3-step plan or easy set of rules—but that's what this book is rejecting anyway. Instead, parents who earnestly and prayerfully desire what is right for their kids (yes, there's that word *desire* again) can help their kids learn to reorder their desires in the same way. Here are a few ideas to get you started.

Tool #1: Teach your child to examine his heart

The first step to learning to desire right is to teach your child to live with a heart that is open to Jesus and with ears that hear Him and His desires. When the "eyes" of the heart are enlightened (Ephesians 1:18), a person becomes spiritually minded and is open to the Holy Spirit examining the desires of the heart. And when a person diligently attends to his own heart issues, he grows less concerned and bothered by worldly issues and less inclined to desire ungodly things. The world simply can't move someone who truly understands how his heart interacts with Jesus.

So how do we teach our child to examine his heart? Early on a child finds ways to protect his heart and learns to use his emotions, thoughts, and behaviors as shields—and even as weapons. He fights when he is frustrated; acts mean when he wishes to be included; withdraws to avoid criticism; puts on a "know it all" attitude to hide deep feelings of inadequacy, or he may even feign an "I don't care" attitude when he fears failure. As a child matures, he needs to learn how to see past these protective layers and be vulnerable and open to the work God wants to do in his heart.

When you observe misbehavior or a habit that isn't in line with what is good, beautiful, or right, the first thing to do may be to have a conversation with your child. Start asking some questions. What is in your heart that makes you feel like this? What is in your heart that makes you want to act like this? What thoughts ran through your head as you made that decision? Patiently talk it through with him, and help him start to see how his desires influence his decisions.

Often a child simply doesn't understand his own desires. Actually, let us rephrase this. Oftentimes, none of us understands our own desires. As adults, we struggle with the same thing. But, start teaching your child about desire at an early age. When your four-year-old desperately wants a Lego set, discuss the desire of his heart. Does he want something to play with? An activity to do with a parent? A new toy to display on his shelf? While none of these are bad things, they can certainly reveal his motivation for that desire. Once your child understands why he desires something, discuss with him why (or why not) that desire is healthy.

Tool # 2: Keep consequences connected to the heart

We've talked a lot in this chapter about how consequences influence head knowledge of what is right and wrong but don't necessarily address heart knowledge. That is true, but that doesn't mean your kids shouldn't have consequences for their behavior—it simply means that the consequences for that behavior should accurately reflect what is going on with the child's heart.

And so, if your three-year-old is struggling to pick up his toys, don't lecture or give time-outs, but simply make these toys unavailable for a while. If your grade-school child keeps forgetting to put away her school uniform, allow her to face the consequences at school when she doesn't wear her full uniform. If your adolescent is talking disrespectfully to you, remove her privilege of seeing friends until she can treat you like she would treat them. These kinds of consequences speak directly to the heart because the child experiences the pain of her own decisions and it places the focus on what's right for her heart...not just on outward obedience.

By providing logical consequences for your children's behavior, coupled with a lot of honest conversation and careful listening, you can help them examine how their desire influences their actions. Thus, they learn to not only change behavior but also reorder their desires.

Tool # 3: Allow your kids to learn from consequences

When a teacher or coach confronts your child or hands down a consequence, resist the urge to defend your child or remove the consequence. Even if you feel he has been mistreated, encourage him to think and advocate for himself. Let your child figure things out and grow from the experience. Be his guide and allow the consequences to help shape his desires. Blaming the teacher, coach, or someone else, takes the focus off your child and places it externally where no shaping of personal desire can take place. Likewise, the child learns to use blame shifting to take the focus off himself.

Tool #4: Avoid instant gratification

Kids often get what they want even before they've had the chance to examine why they want it. And so, a simple way we can help our kids to understand their desires is to make them wait. If your child says she is hungry but she just had a snack, ask her if, maybe, she really just wants something to do. If your teenager wants twenty dollars to buy a shirt *right now*, ask him to work in the yard to earn the money first. If your kids get what they want the instant they want it, you remove from them time to reflect and examine their own hearts and what drives their wants.

Tool #5: Teach children to recognize what is good and what is evil

Since the Garden of Eden, a battle has raged between good and evil. God is good. The devil is evil. We all love stories in which a battle exists between the two, and of course, we love wonderful endings. Symbols of good and evil have existed throughout the ages. Angels are regarded as kind and benevolent. Doves are a symbol of peace. Monsters are regarded as mean. Witches and vampires are evil.

Yet modern literature, movies, and media have changed all this. Witches are no longer evil; they are the good guys. Monsters are heroes. And this can really confuse kids. We must teach them, from an early age, to recognize what is good and what is evil. If they understand the truth, it will connect at a deep level of their hearts with who God has created them to be, and they will not be deceived by the cultural lies they will face.

As educators and authors, both of us are believers in the power of good, quality literature. By exposing young kids to stories that show good winning over evil—and that include examples of wonderful heroes who truly desire God—you're giving them a window into what truth really is.

If you are wondering what books your children should read, a number of authors have done the research for you by compiling lists of excellent pieces of literature for all ages. Here are a few resources we recommend:

- *A Landscape with Dragon - The Battle for Your Child's Mind*, by Michael D. O'Brian

- *Books to Build On - A Grade-by-Grade Resource Guide for Parents and Teachers*, edited by John Holdren and E.D. Hirsch, Jr.
- *A Well Trained Mind - A Guide to Classical Education at Home* by Susan Wise Bauer and Jessie Wise.

Teach them about the heroes of faith by reading to them from the Bible. And as they get older, help them select books that describe true heroes in the history of the world, people who have really made a difference instead of what the pop culture provides. Guide them to want to make a difference for God's kingdom and to desire to do good for others through their own service. This doesn't mean your kids can only read Christian literature—there are hundreds of excellent books that teach about truth and good and evil that aren't necessarily Christian in genre.

Young kids learn the distinctions of good and evil through classical literature such as listed in the references above, in which the good and bad characters are predictably portrayed. In reality however, the distinctions between good and evil characters are blurry. In addition, Satan's plan is to fool us in cunning and deceptive ways. He comes disguised as an angel of light. By adolescence, kids need to be exposed to a variety of complex literature and taught how to discern deceptions as well as the worldviews being espoused. Their ability to discern truth must be sharpened and a powerful way to do this is to *guide them* in the reading of a wide genre of books.

Tool #6: Be patient

Rightly ordered desires form rightly ordered lives and this takes time. It's a process of growth that spans the growing-up years. The process begins with receiving information, responding to it, and then finally owning it. Your elementary-age child is learning the basics of what good character and habits look like. Your adolescent is analyzing the information and likely trying out both good and bad behaviors. By the time she is a young adult, her desires hopefully will be rightly ordered and her character largely characterized by them.

Tool #7: Point your children to the unconditional love of Jesus in your conversations

Only Jesus can transform an innocent heart of a child into a pure heart that will choose, even when no one is looking, to do what is right and good. When your children feel the deep love of Jesus flowing out of your life, they may be irresistibly drawn to Him. This means talking to them about how Jesus has changed you, praying continuously, pointing out Jesus in everything you see and do, and yes, even sharing your own struggles. When they understand how much they are loved by you and by Him, they will be more likely to love Him in return. We love because He first loved us (1 John 4:19). A desire for Him grows out of recognizing His desire for us.

A prayer for desire

Father God, I want my kids to truly know you and your will for their lives. Please, fill them with an inexplicable desire to follow you and your desires—wholeheartedly—and motivate them to do what is right instead of being motivated to simply avoid consequences. Lord, give me the wisdom from You and the words to say so they will see my desire to follow You instead of only the extrinsic motivations of this world. Fill our home with life and with souls that desire you. Amen.

Verses for further study

1 John 4
Psalm 37
1 Corinthians 10:7-13
Matthew 5:6
Proverbs 2:3-5

Chapter 3

REPLACE DISCIPLINE WITH DISCIPLESHIP

(Ellen)

Erika, with tears in her eyes, was standing by the door of my office when I got to work. I sat my coffee on the desk, invited her in, and watched her as she flopped down at the table, her shoulders shaking with sobs. This third-grade teacher and mother to 3-year-old Jesse was undone.

"I just can't get little Jesse to obey! I've tried every discipline trick in the book and nothing works!" Erika moaned.

"Tell me more," I encouraged. And she continued to tell me about the time-outs and the grounding and the spanking and all the things she had tried in her desperation to get Jesse to stay in bed at night. Yet her son—who is definitely "strong-willed"—continued to rule the house as he woke the entire family up at all times of the night.

I think Erika expected me to respond with another tip or trick—a surefire discipline strategy that would make little Jesse stay in his bed like he was supposed to. But I didn't have one, because I've learned that all the discipline strategies in the world will do no good if a child's desire to do wrong is stronger than his desire to do what is right.

So I told Erika to stop disciplining him.

Erika was shocked.

Now, I know full well that Erika would have a midnight cupcake-eating tyrant on her hands if she just let Jesse do what he wanted to do. And that wasn't my suggestion at all. I was simply suggesting that the rote crime-and-punishment discipline that so many parents try (and often fail at) simply doesn't work.

Instead of disciplining them to behave, we have to disciple our kids' hearts to *want* to behave! And that's what our parenting needs to be about—not about control or breaking a child's will or even punishing a crime—but tending to the heart.

That is what I shared with Erika.

But wait! The Bible says...

We know, we know. The Bible says (in Proverbs 13:24) that parents who love their kids are "diligent to discipline" them—and we firmly believe in the inerrancy of the Bible and that God's Word is right and just and true.

But we also assert that when God uses the word "discipline" in the Bible—read Job 5:17, 1 Corinthians 11:32, and Titus 1:8—He uses it to mean what we now consider "discipleship." The word "discipline" (which shares the same root as the word "disciple") means "to chastise, correct, and reprove." In other words, as parents, the Bible tells us we are to guide our children by setting limits and teaching them how to replace bad behavior with good behavior. Yes, we can express disapproval over sin, but we must also encourage, build up, affirm, and gracefully prepare them for the path ahead.

In other words, we are to "disciple" them.

And if we think of discipline as punishment or simply doling out consequences for bad behavior, we lose so much of the deeper things God wants us to give our kids.

The Old Testament Hebrew word for "discipline," *yacar,* refers to both the instruction and correction of children. The New Testament Greek word for child discipline, *paideia,* refers to instruction aimed at increasing virtue. Once we understand this, the aim of discipline is really about the cultivation of the mind and the moral fiber of a child so that he can become all he wants to and is called to become. Discipling your child is about helping him develop a heart after God with Christ-like character rooted within his soul.

Discipleship at its best, reaches deep into the heart—the core of who we are—including our mind and will—the source of our thoughts, feelings, and emotions. The heart is where God does His most profound work, so the heart of a child needs to remain soft so that she is both reachable and teachable.

How we view discipline and what we aim to accomplish by it, plays a significant role in keeping your child reachable and teachable. This must be done with spiritual wisdom and discernment, just as the Holy Spirit responds to us when we sin. In doing so, our correction and reproof will be infused with love, joy, peace, patience, kindness, goodness, faithfulness, gentleness, and self-control—just like Jesus disciples us.

So how exactly is discipleship different from discipline?

My mother is an immigrant from Finland and because my family spoke Finnish at home, I entered first grade with a poor command of English. Fortunately, the school administrator in our small public school also spoke Finnish. Much to my excitement, I discovered that she had the same first name as me. I felt such a connection to her that I began to think that, if I addressed her as "Ellen" and not as Mrs. Vippuri, she would realize our common bond.

I still remember the day when I saw her walking down the stairs of the school and I decided that now was the time. I planted myself at the base of the stairs, and as she ascended, I waved and said, *"Good morning, Ellen!"*

I watched her face turn red, her eyes flashed with anger, and I instantly regretted my actions. She came up to me and shook me by the shoulders yelling, "don't you *ever* address me like that again!"

Embarrassed and ashamed, I climbed the stairs and silently entered the classroom. Any hope of connection between us was shut down for the rest of my days at that school. I avoided Mrs. Vippuri out of fear and shame, and I never told my parents about the incident, worried about what they would think.

I have thought back many times to Mrs. Vippuri. She probably did what she thought was best—to punish what looked, on the surface, like disrespect. She likely never thought of that encounter again, and she surely had no idea how much I would have benefited from reconciliation. Her harsh response only taught me how to show her respect—out of fear.

What if she had possessed a deeper understanding of what it meant to be a godly disciplinarian—one that looked more like discipleship? What if she had understood the common ground that I thought we stood on and from there she gently instructed me about respecting adults? She achieved her immediate goal that day—I never called her Ellen again. But with a grander and higher and more holy aim she could have also gained my genuine respect and a deep connection that would have influenced my heart.

Like Mrs. Vippuri, my dad was a quick-tempered disciplinarian. He was the only attorney in Clatskanie, Oregon and also a cattle farmer. He was a busy man. Time consuming issues with the farm would often fire his temper, especially when he had to brand and castrate calves. On one occasion, my youngest brother came running up to me as I was walking home from school and shouted that Crazy Horn—a feisty, long-horned cow in our herd—had gored my mom.

The trouble started when Dad had Mom stand guard in the field earlier that day while he castrated Crazy Horn's calf. Unfortunately, Crazy Horn charged Mom, goring and kicking her while she lay helpless on the ground. Frightened by the news, I flew into the house, tremendously relieved to find her resting in bed, bruised and cut up, but otherwise okay.

I spent the next two months silently simmering, feeling frustrated with Dad for risking Mom's life. So when Dad asked my brother and me to stand guard as he herded cattle across the road to fresh pastures, I was both angry and afraid.

Dad sternly warned us to stand our ground if any cow tried to escape and not to budge for any reason. I determined to do as he asked—except if Crazy Horn charged—and that was exactly what happened. As Crazy Horn turned in my direction, I leaped out of the way and jumped over a fence. Then I ran, not only from the cow, but also from my dad.

Later, I had to endure his wrath and harsh judgments, and for the first time, I began to distance my heart from him. He apparently had never stopped to think that I might be deeply troubled by the accident with that cow and Mom. He also didn't seem to know that I needed him to care for my safety and that I was too afraid to perform the task he expected of me. So the distance that came between my dad and me was a distance that was magnified over the years, and was still there to some extent until the day he died.

Like Mrs. Vippuri, Dad likely did what he thought was best—to force obedience with a strict hand. But I wonder how differently he would have disciplined his children had he understood the father's role of biblical discipleship. With a discipling approach, my dad might have discovered that my heart's intention was not to defy him. I was simply more afraid of Crazy Horn than I was of his wrath.

Because everything flows from the core of what we believe to be true, how we discipline our kids will reflect those core beliefs. That's why it's so important to comprehend fully the right perspective on how the heart needs to be discipled, not just disciplined. Doing so will not only benefit our children but also breathe life and vitality into the heart of our parenting.

The power of mentoring

Having been raised with an incomplete picture of discipline, I turned to parenting books to deepen my thinking. But it was my close friend and mentor, Kathy, who influenced my perspective the most.

She modeled a discipleship style of parenting with her four children that deeply impacted me. She not only held her children to high standards in all areas, but she also maintained a close, loving relationship with them all along, even through their teen years and beyond.

She would often tell me, "don't listen to anyone who says you can't be close to your teens. It's something you can, and must, purpose to do." Kathy modeled grace-based parenting, yet she also demanded uprightness from her children. So I leaned heavily on her mentorship, and what I saw in her family gave me hope. She dared to go beyond the prevailing thoughts about disciplinary parenting that both the church and secular culture espoused. And she purposed, instead, to maintain relationships with her kids, and in so doing she could influence their hearts.

What about spanking?

Spanking has become one of the major battlefields of parenting in the last two generations—and it's a battlefield that has wounded many on all sides. I raised my kids in an era in which spanking was the "proof" of whether or not a parent employed biblical discipline principles with their kids. I know...that's really sad. But we were largely judged on our ability to parent based on whether we were willing to spank our children.

Now, this generation has become even more divided. There are camps of parents who still firmly believe in spanking, while there are other camps that see it as abusive. The idea of spanking is so polarized that parents on both sides of the fence feel judged and looked down on for their choices. Therefore, spanking is an issue that's often kept under the table, because of the deep-seeded, vehement views on both sides— and because of the pain that divides instead of unites.

So when we started writing this book, we made a very intentional decision not to say "yes" or "no" to spanking. We honestly believe this is an issue between you, your spouse, and God. And there are good parents—good, God-fearing, and loving parents—on both sides of the fence. So we don't want to add to the pain or judgment that already surrounds this issue.

The Bible speaks of the rod of discipline several times in Proverbs. In 1 Corinthians 4:21, the Apostle Paul refers to the "rod" as he addresses the church in Corinth, admonishing them as "his beloved children." He tells them that, although they "have countless guides in Christ, they do not have many fathers," and he says that he has become their "father in Christ Jesus through the gospel." He ends his exhortation in chapter four with, "What do you wish? Shall I come to you with a rod, or with love in a spirit of gentleness?"

This spirit of love and gentleness is very different from a punitive mentality and should replace anger and harshness, which have no place in the discipleship of our children.

We believe that God gives us great discernment when it comes to our kids—and that each parent is given great freedom to parent in a way that works for his or her family. And we further believe that the spirit behind our discipline (or should we say discipleship) is what can truly influence and change our kid's hearts.

TOOLS TO HELP YOU AS YOU DISCIPLE YOUR KIDS

(Erin)

Tool # 1: Offer kids a place to escape

At times, we all need a place where we can let go and vent (just think of the last time your car wouldn't start). Your kids need that too. So, instead of lecturing or punishing your kids for disrespectful talk, tantrums, and whining, simply offer them up a "whine" or "think" rug—a place far away from your ears where they can go to let it all out. Allow them to get off the rug when they are ready to be pleasant and join the rest of the family.

I have a whining corner. My daughter Kate is, well, let's just say she is an avid whiner. Whenever she starts to whine, I simply say "why don't you go whine in the whine corner upstairs?" She goes there, and she usually returns a few minutes later in a much happier state. We both win—the whining (a.k.a. the misbehavior) stops, and she sees me as the one who gave her an escape.

Tool # 2: Give kids a redo

So many young kids make bad decisions in a moment of impulsivity. Just last week, I watched my friend Mary's son, Aiden, walk by his sister and smack an apple out of her hand. The apple was dirty and bruised. His sister was in tears. And Aiden was staring at my friend knowing he was in for it. But my friend wisely gave him a "re-do".

Mary walked up to Aiden, looked him in the eye, and patiently said, "We both know that was wrong, and we both know you knew better, so what happened?"

Aiden's reply? "I wasn't thinking."

"No, you weren't," Mary said. "Let's go back and have a do-over. Then we'll talk about how we can make it better."

So, Aiden took a few steps back and went through the motions of walking by his sister—without smacking the apple out of her hand. Then, Aiden helped her pick up the apple, and they headed to the bathroom together to rinse it off.

Problem solved.

No "discipline."

But a whole lot of discipleship.

Tool # 3: Give kids second chances after a loss of privilege

One Friday night, my husband and I were planning on taking our kids to see a movie after dinner. This was a major treat, and we had been looking forward to it all day. But, at dinnertime, our son Joey was really disrespectful to his dad. I warned him several times, and finally I told him that if he continued to use disrespectful language, he would lose the privilege of the movie.

The last thing I wanted to do was take this special movie outing away from him. But sure enough, two minutes later, Joey turned to his dad and said something like, "you can't make me do what you say." Uh-oh. We had no choice! No movie! My husband chose to stay home with Joey while I took the other kids to the movie, and by the time I got home, Joey was not only repentant, but he was also getting along great with his dad.

The next day, we had a great day. And the next. And the next. And so, a week later, my husband surprised Joey by taking him to a movie— just the two of them. Although some people may say that giving him the privilege at all negated the consequence, I believe that by allowing him the opportunity to earn it back with good behavior showed that we believed in his ability to learn and grow—and proved that we noticed his effort to change.

Tool #4: Give them time

I think back to my psychology class when I learned about Pavlov's dogs and their response to immediate rewards and punishment. The dogs pressed buttons to get rewards. They stopped pressing buttons and got shocked. Monkey see, monkey do.

Do I even need to say this? Our kids aren't dogs *or* monkeys?

Our children don't need immediate punishment or reward to learn a behavior—and it's slightly insulting to think that they do. We need to take the time to address behavior issues with our kids well. We encourage you to spend some time praying and seeking wisdom and discernment *before* addressing an issue.

Even more important, give your kids time alone to ponder their disobedience and repent in their own hearts. Give them time to let God do His work and soften their hearts. Addressing them before their hearts have softened is a waste of time—and addressing an issue out of anger or frustration can be detrimental. Instead, prayerfully and intentionally disciple them as you work through misbehaviors.

Tool #5: Never respond out of anger

(Ellen)

I remember some times when I responded out of anger as a mom—and those are memories that I wish I could forget. Responding to our kids out of anger only exasperates the situation. In James 1:19, the Bible says, "Be quick to hear, slow to speak, and slow to anger, for the anger of man does not produce the righteousness of God."

Our anger will never change our kids! Only God can. And so take the time to allow your anger to calm down before addressing any issue. And, when you are ready, take your child aside (public admonishment will only serve to embarrass), look her in the eye, and have a gentle and wise conversation.

Tool #6: Encourage kids to come up with solutions

When kids misbehave and cause problems, ask them to come up with solutions to problems on their own. Ask them what they can do to fix a certain situation, and if they struggle to come up with an idea, offer suggestions. "Next time you are tempted to talk in class, how can you help yourself remember to be quiet instead?" "When you are tempted to scream with anger, how can you calm yourself down?"

When kids learn that good choices usually bring about good outcomes and bad choices can bring about bad outcomes, they learn cause and effect, and they gain a sense of their own need to develop successful ways to make wise and godly decisions. Nothing is more motivating than feeling the pain of one's own bad choices.

Tool #7: Share your heart

One of the best ways to connect with your kids on a deep level is to share your heart with them. If your child is struggling with something—friendships, organization, honesty, tantrums, disrespect—share with them about a time that you struggled with the same thing and how you overcame it. Knowing that you struggle, too—and that you understand their weakness and were able to successfully walk through it—can give them hope and be one of the best motivators to help them change.

A prayer for discipleship

Father God, give me the words to disciple my children so that they can know You. Remove all pre-suppositions, all of my "oughts" and "shoulds" and help me simply trust You to be all I need to parent my kids. Give me the tools to authentically speak to my kid's hearts instead of simply reacting to their actions. And through these coming years, may they come to see You clearly. Amen.

Verses for further study

Ephesians 6:4
1 Corinthians 4:14-21
1 Corinthians 11:32
Psalm 94:12
Hebrews 12:3-11
Hebrews 4:12

Chapter 4

REPLACE CONTROL WITH CONNECTION

(Ellen)

I watched my grandson Joey as he walked toward the after-school pickup line. I waited for him to give me his usual warm greeting, but instead I saw his downcast, forlorn face. Clearly he was struggling with something.

"What's wrong, Joey?" I asked him.

"Nothing," he said, giving me no eye contact and crossing his arms tightly over his chest. He was obviously upset, and I was not being invited into his pain. I glanced up at his wonderful and caring teacher, and she pulled me aside and told me that he had struggled all day in class. She had tried, multiple times, to break through to him, but he hadn't budged. Instead, he had been rude, disruptive, and angry throughout the entire day.

As his grandmother who lives right next door, I know Joey pretty well. When upset or sad, he tends to act up outwardly. And as an 8-year-old boy, he struggles to understand his negative emotions, other than that they make him feel bad. Then his bad feelings can quickly turn to mad actions. Even bad actions. Then, behaving poorly, Joey's inner turmoil only intensifies, and the cycle goes on to escalate to the kind of day he had that day.

I was tempted to grill him about his actions and force admission of guilt. But I sensed God telling me to gently press him to open up and talk about his emotions instead—to connect with me at a heart level. Initially, my efforts produced more of the same "nothings," but finally, Joey broke down, and with tears streaming down his face, he expressed what was causing his heart such pain.

Joey's Grandpa had suffered a stroke the week before and his dad had flown to see him. Joey was worried about his grandpa and very sad that his dad had left that morning. And he felt like crying.

But boys don't cry. Right?

So all day in class, Joey held in the tears and put his energies into not breaking down. His precious teacher tried to break through his walls. She had noticed Joey's half-heartedness all day. But Joey did not want his teacher to think he was weak. So instead of sharing his honest feelings, he stuffed them and unanswered questions had rolled through his mind.

"What if my teacher doesn't like me if I cry in class?"

"What if my friends make fun of me?"

"Something must be wrong with me to feel this way."

Yet the moment Joey was able to share the source of the sadness he was feeling and his worries over crying, his countenance lifted, and his normal vibrancy returned. Joey just needed someone to connect with him, to believe in him, to listen to him, and to see that he needed a helping hand to pull him up from the despondency he felt inside.

We all—kids and adults alike—need and crave those safe, loving connections with others. When we have people who will *choose* to love us when we are down and out, we see Jesus through them. People who stand by us when we are weary and feeling out of control. When we are wrong. When we fail. When we feel sad. We need to feel understood, respected, and loved.

But all too often, we resort to behaviors that do just the opposite. We try to control. We criticize, argue, blame, and defend. We withdraw. We disconnect. We hide ourselves when we are terrified by what we think others think of us. And we wind up in an emotional whirlwind that pushes our hearts away from others. These negative efforts keep us in a state of emotional disconnection. And disconnected hearts lead to loneliness and disappointment.

What's more, it disconnects us from God.

Our relationship with God isn't contingent on our human relationships, but our human relationships can help us to connect to God in a more clear and meaningful way. God calls on us to be in fellowship with other Christians, and only by forming meaningful and intimate relationships will the love of Christ flow through us and in us. And through these relationships, we can encourage each other, admonish each other, help each other grow, and most importantly, help each other see Jesus.

The moment Joey shared his hurt with me, his face lit up, and just ten minutes later, he was ready to play with his friends again. By taking the time to work through this with Joey, it also allowed me the privilege to teach him about how to handle his emotions. And to show him that it's appropriate to shed some tears at times like this. Even for tough boys!

But I learned something, too. Really, the only true influence I have on Joey—or on anyone—comes through a genuine and loving connection. This same connection is what all people need in order to see Jesus and to learn to love like He does. We are to have compassionate hearts—hearts that are kind, patient, and forgiving. Only out of such hearts can we gain the privilege to teach and admonish one another.

Connection vs. control

Connection and control are contrasting relationship styles. This means that, in relationships, when control is the main motivation, connection is diminished. Likewise, authentic connection diminishes the need to control. This actually plays out in every relationship that we are a part of—marriage, our relationship with our boss, friendships, and yes, even our parenting relationship with our children.

No one wants to be controlled. A boss who over-manages his employees winds up reducing their personal initiative and drives them away because his focus is on outcomes and not on people. A husband who micromanages his stay-at-home wife hurts their relationship because he inadvertently tells her he doesn't trust her to do things on her own.

It's no different with our children. Over-managing them weakens their personal drive as well as impedes their ability to gain their own autonomy and self-control. Overly controlled kids often grow frustrated and defiant, or they come to expect the parent to manage every aspect of their lives because they have little confidence in their own ability to succeed without it. In either case, they eventually find ways to distance themselves and hide what is really going on inside their hearts.

Thankfully, authentic connection between a parent and child opens the parent's eyes to what the child truly needs to grow and thrive as a spiritual and emotional person. The parent's focus is on growing the individual and not controlling the outcomes. As the child gains personal skills, the need to control lessens. Such a parent finds greater satisfaction in standing back and allowing children the time and space to figure things out on their own, understanding how badly that child needs the freedom in order to grow.

Our most important role

(Erin)

As parents, it's so easy to fall into the trap of thinking our most important role is discipline and correction. We hear words like "spare the rod" and "teach them the narrow path," and we start to believe that our number one goal is to manage our kid's behavior. And don't get me wrong, children need guidance and training. But discipline and correction can't come first, because without an authentic heart-to-heart connection, much of what we say will go unheeded. And all our efforts will simply be fueled by control instead of connection, and will yield poor fruit.

A hurt heart instinctively puts up walls. A disconnected heart impulsively withdraws. We must establish a connection that runs from our heart to our child's heart in order to communicate effectively. Otherwise, our communication, whatever it is, largely remains undeliverable.

What if connection with your kids is the first objective in your parenting? What if your days were spent trying to build that connection—having heart-to-heart conversations, spending time on the floor playing, discussing homework, reading books, listening, and praying? Would you spend less time correcting and disciplining? I'd venture to say you would.

Truly knowing someone else

Who *truly* knows you?

This is probably an easy question for most of you. Without thinking you can likely name off two or three people with whom you have formed a close, honest, and deep connection—a relationship where the other person knows you fully and deeply, flaws and all. Whoever it is, in order for us to live fully, we must have at least one or more of these "truly known" connections.

I don't think it's possible to be known by a large number of people. You can be friends with hundreds, but to be known, it takes time and effort and accountability. You simply don't have the time or emotional capacity to form a "truly known" connection with more than a handful of individuals. But those few relationships—well, they should be treasured, cherished, and poured into—and they should be guarded closely.

Our kids need to learn how to form these kinds of deep and meaningful connections, but here's where it gets complicated. As children, our kids simply can't "truly know" us fully—there are too many "adult" things that would not only scare them, but also would be age-inappropriate. Yet as parents, we need to be open and honest about our feelings, hurts, pasts, and personal issues. But we also need to be very cognizant of the reality that there are certain things best left unsaid. Never rely on your children to be your one, true accountable friendship.

With that said, it's important that kids experience being "truly known" in a safe place and at a young age. Model it for them, and allow your home to be a place where they can test the waters of forming deep and meaningful connections by allowing them the space and time to discuss, ask difficult questions, share, and sort through their feelings. Listen willingly, advise only when asked, and show them what a "truly known" relationship looks like so that when they do get older, they will know what it takes to form this type of relationship.

A safe place to land

(Ellen)

In high school, I dated a boy named John. On the outside, John seemed like a stand-up guy. He was funny and athletic and outgoing and smart—and he was captain of the football team. I was a cheerleader. And everyone at school constantly talked about how we were "the perfect couple."

But John and I were far from perfect. John was abusive, controlling, and mean. He would pick me up every morning for school in his gold mustang, and I remember feeling sick as I climbed into the car. As soon as he started down the lane, John would start reminding me of how "fortunate I was" to date him, and he told me how I needed to act in a "deserving way." Which meant I couldn't talk to any other guys. Period.

John's lectures quickly progressed to carefully scrutinizing my clothing—making sure my pants weren't too tight or my shirts weren't too revealing. He'd scream at me if I wore anything that was at all cute or stylish, and he accused me of trying to bring attention to myself by wearing them.

Being 15 and naïve about boyfriends, I simply had no idea that his behavior was really out of line. In fact, one day his behavior fully crossed a line, but I wasn't even sure it was a problem.

That awful day began when we stopped at the local grocery store to get something to drink. I thanked the male checkout clerk, and I guess I must have smiled when I did. John was furious. So on the way home—on a particularly curvy, wooded stretch of the road—he slowed down the car, reached over, opened the door, and shoved me out! Then he drove off, threatening to kill me the next time I "flirted" with any guy.

Fortunately, I wasn't hurt.

But I was ashamed!

Alone and afraid, I started walking toward home, and about a mile down the road, John returned and pulled up beside me. He let me know that "the next time" I would "not be so lucky." He even confessed to me that he'd had a dream about choking me to death!

I was terrified, and I had no one to turn to.

One day I decided to tell my dad about all this, hoping that he would care enough to be my protector and confidant. I ached to have someone connect with me, to understand my fears, my helplessness, my situation. So I sat down and explained what was happening. He nodded and asked questions. He listened to me, and I felt like I finally had an ally, someone who was going to help me.

But, the next day, he didn't say a word about it.

Or the next.

Or the next.

In fact, my dad never brought up our conversation again, and I found out that I really didn't have an advocate. I felt unprotected, and my connection with him was lost.

I was afraid, and I was alone. So I endured John's emotional and physical abuse and his regular manipulation of me silently for nearly two years before he was drafted to go to Vietnam. Somehow I believed I deserved it all and was indebted to him. Sadly, I had no one to tell me differently.

Yet I was fortunate, because in college I met people who understood true connection—one of them being my husband, Glen. These emotionally healthy people wanted to know me, understand me, and give me safety and comfort in being known and protected. With their support, I never spoke with John again, and I learned what it was like to have healthy and connected relationships.

I also vowed to never allow my kids to live in a home where they didn't have a safe place to go in times of trouble. I knew from my experience that kids without a safe place to connect and converse at home often make poor choices when it comes to relationships, and I didn't want that for my children.

Looking back, I think my dad, in his flawed human state, actually thought he *was* a safe place for me to go, even though he clearly wasn't. Likewise, I think a lot of us believe we are a safe place for our kids. But in times of trouble, they often turn elsewhere because we haven't built a heart connection that tells them "no matter what you say or do, I will listen and I will choose to love you."

With this in mind, I want to encourage parents to start building that deep heart connection at an early age—talk, converse, know, learn, grow—so that when your kids are older and have challenges, they will freely turn to you—the ones who know them best.

TOOLS TO BUILD CONNECTION

(Erin)

Tool #1: Daily connection

My friend Julie sets aside 30 minutes every day for each of her kids. During this time, the child can choose what they do—whether it's reading together, playing together, coloring together, or just talking—and the child has her one-on-one undivided attention. I love this idea! And Julie's kids must feel confident that they are a priority to their mom by seeing she has set aside time specifically for them every day.

Logistically, I know this isn't possible for some of you—with multiple kids and work demands, setting aside 30 minutes a day may be impossible. But could you set aside 10? Or dedicate one Saturday a month to do something specifically that builds your connection with your kids? I think you would find that it's not only worth it, but also fun.

Tool #2: Connect with conversation

Think about the conversation around your dinner table. If it's anything like ours, there are days where it sounds something like this:

"How was your day?"

"Fine. Yours?"

"Oh, fine. Johnny in HR told me that they are getting lots of good applicants for the new position."

"That's nice."

And it goes on. And on. Days go by without anyone really getting to know anything real or meaningful about anyone else. We simply can't waste this time! I encourage you to make your conversations intentional. That means you make it a point to discuss real topics, ask important and detailed questions, and work hard to get to know each other—on a deeply emotional and spiritual level.

Here is a list of questions to get you started:

1. What was the best thing that happened to you today? How did it make you feel?
2. Who is one person you prayed for today? What did God reveal to you?
3. What is one thing you would change about today?
4. Who has God placed on your heart today?
5. Did you do anything that made you feel energized today?
6. Did you do something that helped you to work toward a goal?
7. Tell me about a conversation you had today that made you think about something important.
8. Tell me about something you saw today that made you want to learn more.
9. Tell me how you felt when you woke up. Did the day meet your expectations?

Tool #3: Set an example

Your kids learn what they know about relationships from the relationships they observe. If you aren't working hard to form an intimate connection with your spouse, you are inadvertently showing your kids that connection isn't important. Model the importance of deep connection. Let your kids see you having intimate conversations, talking about what really matters, praying together, and supporting each other so they can begin to understand what true connection looks like.

It's also important for your kids to see intimate connections in all of your relationships. That means intentionally choosing to deepen your relationships with your kids and your spouse as well as with your Christian friendships. Show your kids that you value community, relationship, and even accountability, so that they can, in turn, learn to build similar relationships for themselves.

Tool #4: Focus on the process instead of the outcome

(*Ellen*)

Outcomes matter, and you should be happy for your kids when they get great grades, place well in a race, or get the lead role in the play. But if we spend all our time focusing only on outcomes, then we ignore the important process through which we can connect with them. Our kids need to see our acceptance and love when they struggle and things don't go well, and they need to know that we value them unconditionally, even if they aren't the best at whatever they are doing. It's important that your connection with your kids is constant, especially when they need it the most. They need to see that your emotions don't go up and down with their performance. If we fluctuate with their ups and downs, it puts too much pressure on them to get the outcomes that please.

The way to avoid this tendency is to pay attention to the learning process—pray for her, notice her effort, and connect with your kid while she studies for the test or practices for the soccer game. Make statements like "I noticed that you've been practicing really hard to improve your free throws" versus "you made the most free throws in the game." This keeps your focus on what is most important—that she is learning and growing—and off what matters less—the outcome. More important than the grade she receives or the accomplishment she achieves is how hard she worked or how she improved through the process. A focus on the process of learning and growth not only helps your child maintain a strong ongoing process—which is what leads to success—but it also keeps your connection with her intact regardless of the outcome.

Tool #5: Improve your body language

Kids know when you are listening—or not listening—by your body language. Be intentional about listening to your kids when they are telling you something that is important to them. Take the time to get at their level and listen not only with your ears but also listen with your eyes by looking directly at them. Eye contact builds connection. We communicate a lot through body language whether it's our disinterest or impatience, or it's what we delight in or approve of. Though it's a lot to think about all at once, continue to work at effectively communicating—not only with your words but also with your body.

A prayer for connection

Father God, You aren't a pie-in-the-sky God who rules from afar, but instead, You are the Author of love and of relationships. You are not only the Creator of the universe, but You know me personally and intimately. Lord, thank You for knowing me and loving me. I pray that I can follow Your example and form an intimate, real, and safe connection with those I love. Give my kids comfort in the fact that they are truly known, not only by You, but by other people who love them in spite of their faults.

Lord, give me patience, forgiveness, longsuffering, kindness, and hope in my relationships so that I can be like You. Amen.

Verses for further study

John 15:13
Proverbs 18:24
Hebrews 10
Ephesians 4:2-3
1 Peter 1:3-5

Chapter 5

REPLACE COMPLACENCY WITH GROWTH

(Erin)

Right after my son Joey turned five, he came downstairs, dressed in a polo shirt, slacks, dress shoes, and he was carrying his Buzz Lightyear backpack. He proudly announced to me that he was ready to go to Kindergarten. He had been told that five-year-olds go to Kindergarten—and now that he was five, he was ready. Never mind that it was late December and school wasn't even in session.

I explained to Joey that he had to wait until after the summer to start kindergarten, but then I informed him that he could start learning now. Those simple words lit a fire in him. For the next several months, he didn't want to play trucks or cars or superheroes; instead, he wanted to play school.

This has continued, even to today.

He's now in second grade, and he often begs me to "tell him something interesting." He spends hours reading non-fiction books about topics like tornadoes or giant gorillas or the history of the printing press. He craves facts. He desires to succeed. And he's willing to spend his time and energy to do just that.

This interest in learning is actually typical of kids his age. Most young kids have an innate desire to learn and grow—yet often, by the time these same kids are ten or eleven, this desire fades. These same kids—the ones who begged to learn "something else interesting" do an about-face and stop desiring growth and start desiring complacency.

Why do so many Christian kids stop learning and growing? Most set out with good intentions, some with lofty ones to "change the world." But if they are not personally growing and changing within, they will find themselves "stuck in a ditch" instead.

I can tell you all of the standard answers—it's because of sin or disobedience or the pervasive impact of our culture. But perhaps there is a better answer. Perhaps we need to open our eyes to what is missing—to what is needed for steadfast growth in each of our kids.

Jesus wants us to grow and to keep on growing our entire lives. But so often something gets in the way, and we stop growing. The truth is that personal growth has less to do with our circumstances than it has to do with everything else that dims the eyes of our hearts. A heart that sees Jesus is intuitively able to discern the impact of today's choices on tomorrow's success. And with this discernment, we can have the courage to walk forward, to learn, to grow and to stretch. We can have the courage to become one who is willing to step forward and stand for truth—even when the culture is sinking in mediocrity.

This is a heart that grows. And we must help our children learn how to cultivate an ever-growing heart.

Avoiding the Trap of Complacency

(Ellen)

I enjoy observing how my own adult kids parent their children. Currently, my kids have three children each, and as they raise their families, they are learning what I once learned—that each child is different. Even siblings reared in the same house with the same parents and the same rules are so very dissimilar. Their unique personalities come equipped with vastly different outlooks and approaches to life.

But each and every child needs to maintain a heart that grows and changes—or they risk growing complacent instead.

Complacency is the opposite of growth. So let's look at the many characteristics that lead to complacency and stop kids from growing, and understand how to counter this downward spiral.

Tendencies that lead to complacency:

1. *Fear:* The thought of getting hurt, or possibly failing, makes it scary to risk trying. Fear makes kids come up with all sorts of reasons why they shouldn't even begin.

2. *Competiveness:* While a competitive nature can motivate someone to accomplish a lot, children who focus on other's growth and success instead of their own are often blind to the areas where they need to grow themselves.

3. *Perfectionism:* Children who are scared to make mistakes are often unwilling to try if the outcome could potentially be less than desired. This leads to a complacent "I don't care" attitude that hinders growth. (By the way, this is one of my favorite topics, and I have spent countless hours researching perfectionism and how we can help our kids get past it. If you have a perfectionistic kid, please visit my blog at www.familywings.org and search "perfectionism" for more information.)

4. *People Pleasing:* People pleasers are constantly wondering what others are thinking. And whether they are happy. And how they can win their approval. And this others-focused striving stands in the way of true growth. If self-worth is based in what others think, they become enslaved to pleasing and performing. These kids are no longer free to grow into the people God has created them to be.

5. *Over protection:* Kids who are not expected to solve their own issues or figure out how to overcome obstacles, come to feel that they are incapable. They get used to the idea of letting other people do their hard work for them and fail to gain skills themselves.

6. *Lack of challenge*: Without sufficient challenge, kids will not experience the joy of victory. When kids discover purpose in tough times, the difficulties transform into opportunities and growth occurs.

What does learning and growing have to do with Jesus?

What does all this talk about learning and growing have to do with kids and their faith in God? A lot. Young children often start out excited about learning the "rules" of faith. They soak up the Sunday school lessons like a sponge. They sing worship songs. They learn Bible stories. They can easily spout off lots of "Christianese." They learn that shouting the name "Jesus" brings a robust response. At a young age and with a childlike faith, most are enthusiastic about the Gospel.

But as time passes, kids figure out how to put their knowledge into practice only when they are in the spotlight—when adults are looking. But, it's what they choose to do in the "shadows"—when no one is looking—that shows how authentic their faith is becoming.

A lot of kids spend more and more time in the "shadows" as they progress through their educational years—and today's ever increasing media sites grant them even easier access to "shadowy" places out of the view of adults. Sadly, they eventually let go of their identity with Christ and reach for a host of temptations that the world offers. They develop an impulsive and self-absorbed lifestyle, and they too often find themselves no longer running the race of faith. The vision (and hope) for the future they once had fades and pleasing themselves and their peers becomes their main objective.

In this world, where complacency is almost expected, we must equip our kids to practice their faith and continue to want to grow instead of allowing our kids to sink into stagnate habits. By doing this, we give our kids a huge advantage, not only in their academic, athletic, and artistic pursuits, but also in their spiritual ones.

One step at a time

(Erin)

Have you ever made homemade sourdough bread or pancakes or waffles? If not, let me explain sourdough to you.

Sourdough can be a bit complicated. First, you have to make a sourdough starter by fermenting flour. This gives its sour flavor. This starter can last years; I know of someone who has passed a sourdough start down for generations. It lasts as long as it's "fed" a little bit of sugar every few days. I once kept a sourdough starter in my fridge for years, stirring it occasionally, feeding it frequently, and enjoying the flavor it added to baked goods. The great thing about sourdough is that, once you have a good starter, making sourdough-baked goods is easy. Just add starter to your batter, and it gets that amazing sourdough flavor.

You can also share the love and give your friends and family members a scoop of your starter (which will quickly replenish itself), and they can start their own. Cool, right? (Note: If you want to make your own sourdough starter, you can find full instructions at www.familywings.org/sourdoughstarter.)

The reason I'm telling you this isn't to get you interested in baking, but instead to illustrate a point. A sourdough starter has to grow—or it dies. If you feed it sugar, add water, and stir it occasionally, it thrives for years, adding life to your baking. But if you neglect it, even for a short period of time, it stagnates, and within days, it can go bad. It turns from a delicious addition to your baked goods to a slimy, moldy mess.

Our kids are the same. (Well, except for the slimy, moldy mess part.) Growth is rarely seen as big, drastic changes to who they are, but instead, we usually observe a series of small changes over a period of time. And like starter, for kids to grow, they need to be fed daily—through our encouragement, prayer, support, conversation, and connection. (Get it? Like the sugar in the sourdough starter.) And, finally, once they start to grow and change, these changes can last a long time, and they can even spread to other areas of their lives, influencing not only their own path, but also the paths of those around them.

Challenges lead to growth

(Ellen)

Some of the greatest athletes in the world have had to overcome major obstacles. I think of Wilma Rudolph, who was not only paralyzed by polio but was also stricken with scarlet fever and double pneumonia. Her doctors said she would never walk again. Yet she not only regained her ability to walk, but eight years later, through hard work and therapy, she became an Olympic champion who would set three world records. I wonder if she would have achieved as much without working through the difficult circumstances she had to overcome!

None of us want to see our kids struggle, so it's natural for us as parents to do whatever we can to remove the very challenges our kids need to help them learn and grow. We often retreat from what frightens them—or from what frightens us. Yet we should teach our kids that challenges, and the discomfort (within reason) that comes with them, is part of the normal process of growth.

Learning to ride a bike is uncomfortable, at first. *"What if I fall and get hurt?"* Taking a test is uncomfortable. *"What if I fail and look dumb?"* Jumping off the blocks to race in a swim meet can be frightening for a beginner. *"What if I come in last?"* Performing in one's first piano recital can be terrifying. *"What if I forget the notes?"*

If you hear one of these phrases coming from your child's lips, would your gut reaction be to save her from the stress? Would you want to tell her she didn't have to do it if she weren't ready or intervene in some way to help her avoid the challenge? I think most parents (if answering honestly) would have that inclination. But we have to work hard as parents to resist it.

Kids need to understand that to achieve success in anything—big or small—requires the willingness to take a risk—and to sometimes even fail. Every challenge has an element of discomfort—that's just life. But each time your child faces a challenge, and grows through the experience, his confidence takes a leap as well.

I can only imagine the hard work that Wilma Rudolph went through to grow from a sickly, crippled, young girl to an Olympic Champion. Her journey undoubtedly included a heaping dose of pain, discouragement, and struggle. But she did not give up.

Growth is a lifetime journey

When I look back, I see how my greatest growth has occurred during challenging times, whether physically, mentally, emotionally—or spiritually. If you are like me, it's in the easy stretches of my journey that I quit growing and become complacent. There are times that it feels far easier to remain comfortable and complacent than to face my fears and to grow. That's human nature. But every time I back down from moving forward, I find myself becoming sidetracked from the real desires of my heart.

It's in the tough and challenging stretches of the race of my spiritual life—when I long for living water to sustain me—that I maintain my forward movement. In James 1, it says "Count it all joy, my brothers, when you meet trials of various kinds. For you know that the testing of your faith produces steadfastness." And I've found that as I struggle, as I am forced to press in and lean into our most holy God, the greatest changes take place in my heart. It is then I see His glory, my own pride fades, and I get out of His way.

My 86-year-old mom has Alzheimer's, a disease that is slowly destroying her mind. I wonder how she can still grow? How do I reach her and ease her anxiety? Then God gently reminds me to pray with her and point her to Him. He is all she needs to comprehend in this final leg of her journey. As everything around her grows dim and confusing, she needs to see His light more than ever. Her mind isn't growing anymore, but her hold on God can grow stronger as her hold on the world falters.

Matthew 7:13, 14
"... For the gate is wide and the way is easy that leads to destruction... For the gate is narrow and the way is hard that leads to life..."

Growth, pure and simple, is hard work but it's also life giving.

Growth promotes growth

Growth and change is invigorating, and God created us to grow and change more and more, especially into His likeness, throughout our entire lives. In fact, growth fuels more growth. But the same is true in the reverse. When we don't grow, we become complacent. One way or the other, we are moving in some direction. Either we are growing, or we are growing stagnant.

You and I need the same things children need to keep growing and learning. We need wise boundaries and a self-controlled mind to keep us focused on what is important. We need to face our fears in the face of challenges, and we need to remain teachable and humble. We need to look upward to Jesus and not outward in an effort to please or compare ourselves to others. It's Jesus who brings life to what is dying inside us!

The path of growth, and ultimately of becoming pure (like Him), is arduous. Jesus gives us a new heart, but then we have a huge role to play in the formation of who we become—of growing healthy, godly habits and character. And much of it has to do with the decisions we make, the steps we take each day, that move us in one direction or in another. In the final analysis, the quality of our lives will be determined by the growth toward purity of our hearts. And the only path to a pure heart is to pursue and to keep our eyes on Him throughout the journey.

TOOLS TO HELP KIDS GROW

So how can you practically help your kids learn to reject complacency and desire growth in a world where kids are often encouraged to maintain the status quo and to do the bare minimum? Here are a few tips:

Tool #1: Pray affirmatively instead of giving lectures

When you pray with your kids, have you ever caught yourself saying something like *"God please help Tommy to remember to be honest,"* or "Lord, please help Sally to learn patience." This isn't helpful! It's a kind of "pray-lecturing." Try switching it up, and praying affirming words over your kids. Try: *"Lord I thank you that Tommy is learning to be honest and on his way to becoming a man of integrity,"* or *"Thank you that Sally was able to patiently wait for me today while I was cooking dinner."* Such affirming words offer hope because they paint a vision for who they are becoming.

Tool #2: Don't remove the challenges

If you catch yourself wanting to intervene when your kids face challenges, stop and consider the long-term consequences of them taking the easier path before making a decision. None of us like to see our kids struggle, and we want them to be happy. Yet the path to true joy and learning comes through struggle. Just because something is hard, does not mean it isn't worth it. Teach your kids early on that the hardest tasks are often those that are the most fulfilling. Free yourself from the unnecessary weight of seeing your kid's struggles and challenges as your own. Focus your energies instead on coaching them from the sideline, allowing them to learn and grow.

Tool #3: Focus on the process

It's easy to focus on outcomes—grades, awards, assessments, and achievements. They not only make our children feel good, but they also make us feel successful as parents.

However, outcomes are simply products of the process; a signal of what has occurred along the way to growth. Good daily decisions usually result in good outcomes, and the reverse is also true. Outcomes summarize the process of growth that has been happening all along.

A swimmer who works hard at practice day in and day out will improve her times. A basketball player who refuses to listen to the coach during practice will likely get less playing time during the game, because he won't understand the plays and hasn't done the work to prepare for the game. It's important to focus your attention on the process of growth by showing your kids specifically *how* they need to grow—whether in effort, neatness, paying attention, or simply not giving up.

Tool #4: Praise the process, not the kid

Focus your praise on the process as well. *"I noticed you worked extra hard to make that artwork colorful,"* versus *"You are such a great artist—you deserve first place."* Focus your praise more on character and on the fruits of the spirit. *"I love how gentle you are with the younger children,"* or *"I am grateful that you chose to be kind to your little sister."*

Avoid letting your child get caught up in the cultural lie that "kids who are good at something are that way "naturally." Praises such as *"you are so bright—you got an 'A' without studying,"* give a child the unintended message that, "bright kids don't have to study, and only kids who are not very smart really need to work hard." The same is true with being good at sports, music, art, or anything.

If something is hard at first, don't assume it is not for your child. It takes practice and hard work to become accomplished at almost anything. But today, there's an insidious anti-growth message that says,

"If at first they don't succeed, then quit." Don't buy it! Instead, praise your child for hanging in there and doing something that does not come easily.

Also, keep your praises realistic and not lofty. Kids know when your praise is unearned flattery, and you want them to trust that what you say is true and right. If you say he is "the best soccer player on the team," but the coach does not play him as if he is, then someone is either lying or lacks poor judgment. You don't want that label on you! Moreover, he may not want you to watch his games for fear that you will learn the truth. Bottom line is, be sincere, truthful, and affirming, take the high road instead of the easy road, and help your child to want to keep on growing.

Tool #5: Normalize discomfort

Growing and learning feels uncomfortable because it stretches us. Teach your kids that this type of discomfort is normal and to be expected. When your son is confused about a math concept and wants to quit working, remind him that the struggle he feels is a part of the process of learning and growing. When your daughter is experiencing conflict with a friend, tell her it's normal to feel discomfort over conflict, but she should still address the issue, and figure out how to manage the clash well.

Tool #6: Be empathetic and understanding

An empathetic, understanding attitude on your part is the best means by which to give your child the support and reassurance they need to keep going. You don't have to agree with them to understand how they are feeling. You can empathize with their struggles without removing the pain. To know that someone understands and feels badly for the pain one is experiencing is often all that is needed to be reenergized.

Tool #7: Allow plenty of opportunities to choose and make decisions

Making wise decisions is a vital skill, one that determines direction. That's why kids need plenty of practice when poor decisions have smaller consequences so that they learn from their mistakes while it's relatively easy to still change directions. The way down is always open, easy to sink in, but difficult to climb out. And the downward path pulls harder and harder the lower they plunge.

The first poor decisions can feel like no big deal at the time. Lazy judgments. Acceptable compromises. Minor disobedience. In hindsight however, how differently would they (we) choose, if they had known where those first few decisions would lead?

Kids naturally want plenty of freedom and the right to make their own choices. They prefer however not to own the outcomes of their own poor decision-making. Why not have mom or dad pay for the textbook they lost or the ticket they got for speeding? In order to grow in their responsibility to govern themselves however, they need to first understand that the freedom to choose does NOT come with freedom from the consequences. The truth is that nothing will help them grow more in individual responsibility than to experience the outcome of their own decision making. Only then will they actually be able to enjoy freedom anyway!

Tool #8: Teach kids to fully engage in both work and play

Hadassah, one of my five grand daughters, fully engages in life. I rarely see her when she is not fully invested in whatever she is doing. When she is happy, she bubbles over with enthusiasm. When she is sad, she melts into a puddle. Entirely. Whether it's swimming with her cousins or taking Irish dance lessons, Hadassah pours all of her energy into life. As a five-year-old, she is already growing and gaining many good skills as a result. Complacency will likely not become an issue for her. On the other hand, I see many students today who choose to partially engage and soon lose interest in learning because they are not experiencing growth and change. When kids learn what it feels like to fully engage in what they are doing however, whether it's schoolwork, athletics, music, or art, they experience the intrinsic joy in improving and growing.

A prayer for growth

Lord, it's so easy for us to stagnate. I want so badly to constantly grow closer to You, but instead I find myself floundering, complacently waiting in the murky places of life without seeing growth. Lord, remove that from me. Help me to wake up each day with a burning desire to grow—in godliness and knowledge and faith and trust and hope and all the other good things You have for those who love You. And Lord, I want the same for my kids. Give me the tools to help them grow in a way that honors You and helps them to reach the full potential of who You want them to be.

Verses for further study

Matthew 17
Psalm 1
Ephesians 4:14-16
James 1
2 Peter 1:5-8
Philippians 1:9-11

Chapter 6
REPLACE LECTURES WITH LOVE

[Ellen]

Erin, my oldest (and co-author of this book), was the most challenging to raise of all my kids. I joke that if God had given me my even-tempered son first, I probably would have written that parenting book when I was twenty-two. After all, with him, I did it all right.

But with Erin, things were an uphill struggle from day one, and it took me years to figure out why. I felt we had all the pieces in place for a great mother-daughter relationship. I loved her. I had read every parenting book on the market. I listened to Dr. Dobson on the radio. I gave her educational opportunities. I spent time with her. Everything seemed idyllic. Yet we were constantly butting heads.

When something would go wrong with her—whether a fight with a friend, a low grade at school, or a mistake on a test—I would swoop in like the quintessential "good" mom and do whatever it took to help her fix it. I wanted to help her learn to solve her own problems, and I'd point out a way for her to improve, or I'd help her to see the mistake she had made so she could do better next time. But instead of responding positively to my suggestions, Erin would often fall apart.

What I failed to see—for years—is that, what looked to me like an unwillingness to hear criticism was not that at all. Instead, at a deeper level, Erin lived under the fear of losing my approval and love! A mistake made her feel unloved. A criticism made her feel unworthy. And when she felt unloved and unworthy, Erin would spiral down, sometimes out of control.

Ugly words would fly. We would argue. Then we would both retreat. And, finally, we both ended up feeling unwanted, unloved, and incapable of doing right. Finally I learned how to deal with my daughter in a more productive way and see that she simply needed to know my unconditional love and approval—instead of only hearing criticism.

After experiencing many of these sad and hurtful episodes—after which both of us had said things we never meant to say and would still do anything to take back—I began to realize a different way.

I was desperate to respond differently and in my desperation, I prayed for help. God's response seemed almost too simple, but after contemplating it for a while, I realized that I was learning a profound truth: In order to love our kids like Jesus does, we have to love them *in* their messiness instead of in spite of it!

So I started to be intentional about showing that I loved her—like Jesus would. I learned how to speak to her in more affirming ways. I chose to set aside my "I-must-fix-this" attitude, and instead, I determined to show her that I loved her and supported her through all her mistakes. I had to become the hands and feet and mouth of Jesus and love my precious daughter in a way that she could "see" Jesus' love—and mine!

I remember a time when, as a young adult, Erin was experiencing a particularly tough season. But rather than affirm her, I fell back into the "let me tell you what you did wrong" habit. As Erin began to spiral down in response to my old methods, I quickly realized my mistake—I wasn't showing her the acceptance she needed. That day was a wake-up call to never forget to put her needs before my natural inclinations.

In Romans 8:38-39, we learn that we can do nothing that will ever separate us from Christ's love. That's a powerful statement, and one that many of us don't fully comprehend. Nothing—nothing on this earth or outside of this earth—no situation, no mistake, no sin—will ever separate us from the love of Christ. And nothing will separate our kids from the love of Christ, either.

It's a biblical truth, but many of us unknowingly model just the opposite for our children. I didn't intentionally model conditional love for Erin, but that's exactly what I did. As parents, we too often model a love that's conditional, and in doing so, our kids never learn to fully accept Christ's love. We model a love that judges, that corrects, and that complains. In doing so, our kids never learn to understand God's unconditional spirit of love.

Matthew 22:37 says that the greatest commandment is to "love the Lord your God with all your heart and with all your soul and with all your mind." This is impossible if we don't first comprehend His love for us. If our hearts are not first immersed and secured by His love, then we will not be able to love Him back. And we will never be able to fully love the people God places in our lives. That includes our children. We must *know* God's love first.

The one who is secure in God's love will love in return.

Loved ones love.

After years of struggling to learn how to show love to my oldest daughter, I finally realized that the best thing I can offer her—or anyone—is to continually model for her the type of love that God has for her. We give our kids a wonderful inheritance when we help them to fully understand God's love. And, in doing so, we give them the ability to love others in the way that God calls us to.

By accepting God's perfect love for us, we can model that kind of love for our kids in a way they can understand, accept, and embrace. We can teach them, not only to love others, but also to allow God's love to seep deep into their entire being and transform them into His image and likeness as they grow and mature.

Teaching our kids about God's perfect love

(Erin)

I'm the first to admit that I don't fully understand God's love. Who does? I think it's impossible for us as humans to fully comprehend the perfect love of a perfect God. We just can't fathom how wide it is, or imagine how deep it is, or believe how full it is or grasp how complete it is.

Real agape love is incomprehensible. Our intellect can never really figure out who God is because He is unlike anyone or anything else. "Left to ourselves we tend immediately to reduce God to manageable terms," wrote A.W. Tozer in his book, *The Knowledge of the Holy*. "We need the feeling of security that comes from knowing what God is like."

There are so many facets of God's love that it would take a lifetime to even begin to contemplate it all. But we should try! While spiritual maturity requires that we grow out of our childish ways, we should never, ever lose a childlike heart that yearns for the tender, yet fierce love of our Father in Heaven.

In fact, try it right now—yes, put down this book and go grab your Bible. Spend a few minutes—or hours if you get carried away—writing down ways that God loves us. The list is infinite, but here are a few:

- Our God—the One who is completely perfect—considers us His inheritance. Yes, we are God's inheritance. The God who created and who rules the entire universe has chosen us to be His children and to live with Him forever (Ephesians 1:18).
- He not only desires good things for us, but He is also constantly working for our everlasting welfare. We may not always know why things happen the way they do, but God uses all things for our good and to make us more like Jesus (Romans 8:28-29).
- God desires a deep and meaningful relationship with us. Abraham dared to claim that, "I am a friend of God," and God honored that. God wants to be your best friend, your confidant, your source of strength, and your source of hope (Isaiah 41:8).

- God takes pleasure in us. He smiles when we smile, He laughs when we laugh. We share His joy as we experience Him in a deeper and more meaningful way (Psalm 104).

And the list goes on and on.

What a wonderful reassurance and hope we have—that the living God, the creator of the universe, loves us like that. And even though not one of us can fully comprehend His love, every little glimmer of understanding it allows us to, in turn, love others better. This means that the more we teach our kids about God's love, the more they will be able to relate to others like God does—with patience, with a servant's heart, with respect, with kindness, with forgiveness, and with hope.

Isn't that what we want for our kids? I sure want it for mine. And I pray that they will grow, every day, in understanding God's perfect love, and in turn, use that understanding to better love others.

But that's not an easy process—and it must come *from* God. Human love is simply flawed. So as much as I love my kids, I have to trust that God loves them even more, and His love is all that can ultimately satisfy their hearts.

Modeling a love that mirrors Jesus

If there is one thing I know about parents, it's that they love their kids. I've never heard a mom say, "well, I held him for the first time and I just felt sort of ambivalent," or "I used to love him, but then he hit the terrible twos and that just went away." The thought is laughable. Of course we love our children.

The problem is that we are all flawed, and because of this, the unconditional love we feel for our children is also flawed. We sometimes lose patience. We aren't always kind. We don't forgive, we aren't slow to anger, we aren't generous, we aren't longsuffering.

But Jesus is.

And if we want our kids to learn to love like Jesus does, we have to model Jesus's love.

True, this isn't easy. We are imperfect people—but people who are loved perfectly by a perfect God. None of us can completely love like Jesus does. But we can certainly try—and every bit of love we share with our kids gives them another glimpse into the perfect love that their Creator has for them.

Expressing the love of Jesus

(Ellen)

As parents, we are tasked with the divine work of expressing God's love to our children and a powerful way we can do this is to communicate delight in them. Delighting in your kids is key in gaining access to their hearts because delight expresses love and love dispels fear.

My parents seemed to be too busy managing life to find pleasure in their children. Perhaps the thought never really occurred to them that showing delight, or telling us they loved us, would have been powerfully motivational. We didn't need praise or flattery, but it would have done our hearts good to know they enjoyed us and found pleasure in who we were. Their expressions towards us were more about how we displeased and disappointed them however, which prevented me from opening up my heart to them.

Focus on what delights you about each of your children instead of feeling trapped by all that displeases you. You may see your three-year-old as a tornado causing havoc wherever he goes, but show appreciation for his passion and his creative expression. Your adolescent may walk in the house disappointed in the events of the day, but delight in her willingness to open up and share her heart with you. Make sure your eyes light up when she first sees you, to acknowledge that you are glad to see her. Take time to discover each child's unique interests, passions, and what motivates them as well as what discourages them. Consider their input and listen to their thoughts and dreams. Really listen! Hidden in each child are gems waiting to be discovered and polished and the more you look for them, the more these gems will begin to sparkle. So purpose to delight in your kids so that they won't have to fill this deep need elsewhere!

TOOLS TO TEACH KIDS ABOUT HIS LOVE

We firmly believe that only a heart that is loved by God really knows how to love well and here are a few tools that can help you teach your kids to accept His love fully.

Tool #1: Scripture and prayer

Earlier in this chapter, we suggested you do an exercise where you spend time in the Scripture reading about all the ways that God is love. Wouldn't this be a great thing to do with your kids or as a family? Perhaps you could have each child find a Scripture about Christ's love and then pray that Scripture over the family out loud at breakfast. Or maybe you could chart all the ways the Bible talks about God's love. However you do it, I want to encourage you to prayerfully and intentionally use Scripture to teach your children about love from an early age.

Tool #2: A quiet spirit

Learning from my less-than-loving experiences with my oldest daughter, I've discovered that a quiet spirit is usually a loving spirit. I often tell parents to just zip their lips when dealing with a child who is angry or hurt or frustrated. In the moment, all that matters to the child is proving that the parent is wrong. If the parent tries to prove that the child is wrong, the entire process of growth gets off track and stuck in a muddy, gooey mess.

The truth is that hurt, frustrated people feel unloved and unworthy. And the best way to treat someone who is feeling that way is to love him like Jesus would. So, next time your child is hurt, frustrated or angry, love him. Hug him, listen to him, hold him, and connect with him. I'm not telling you to love or excuse the sin. Instead, patiently and quietly show him that you love him regardless of what he has done.

Tool #3: Words that communicate love

Think about your communication with your child. Do your words and body language regularly communicate:

- Lecture or loving guidance?
- Frustration or patience?
- Disappointment or acceptance?
- Criticism or correction?
- No or yes?
- Inconvenience or enjoyment?
- Judgment or acceptance?

Words are powerful, and as you talk with your kids—whether it's about a major issue or an everyday happening—think about how your words communicate love—or not. It's easy to get caught up in the craziness of a day and inadvertently communicate to our kids that we don't have time to stop and listen. And it's easy to get caught up in the moment and communicate criticism instead of unconditional love. Prayerfully consider your words, your tone, and your communication so that you show your kids a Christ-like love with everything you say and do.

A prayer for loving acceptance

Loving Father, You are unchanging. Your everlasting love for me is my hope. Lord, I want to grow closer to you as I raise my kids and in doing so, help them to grow closer to you. Help me to love them deeply in a way

*that resembles your perfect love. Give me the discernment to know when
to talk, when to listen, and when to just be. Amen.*

Verses for further study

1 John 4
Romans 8
1 Corinthians 13
Psalm 139:13-18
Isaiah 49:15-16
Ephesians 2:4-5
Titus 3:4-5

Chapter 7

REPLACE ANGER WITH FORGIVENESS

(Ellen)

Erin and I firmly believe that forgiveness is one of our highest human needs. Without genuine forgiveness, there can be no security in our relationships—either with God or with others. And without security, we are unable to safely draw near to those we need the most when we are struggling. This often causes us to be bitter, ineffective, and angry.

I have watched a lack of forgiveness destroy the life of someone I am very close to, leading her to self-destruct into a life full of bitterness, angst, and pain. I grew up with Jane, and she was a sweet child. She was kind, loving, and caring, often going out of her way to help others. She was also the one her parents called "the good one," or "the perfect one," often overlooking her misbehavior or blaming it on her siblings. Jane figured out early on that big batting eyes and a "who me?" grin could get her out of almost any bit of trouble.

As she grew up, Jane's adorable nearly perfect smile got a little less cute. She found out quickly that her teachers wouldn't let her get by with things that her parents had overlooked. And when she wasn't around her parents or siblings, there was no one to blame when things didn't turn out as she had hoped. She started to spiral out of control, getting angry when things didn't go her way, and searching desperately for someone to blame when she was in trouble.

Before long, Jane let herself feel hurt when others didn't see her as "perfect" like her parents did. So instead of releasing this pain through conversation, conviction, redemption, and then forgiveness, Jane clung to it. She cut out any relationship where she felt even the least bit of strife.

For Jane, unresolved strife led to bitterness, and by the time she was in college, Jane struggled in all her relationships. She would meet someone new and things would go well for a while, but as soon as something faltered—the other person didn't meet her expectations or there was a disagreement—Jane cut that person out. By the time Jane reached adulthood, her relationships with everyone in her life were splintered.

To this day, this pattern of bitterness and unforgiveness has continued. Jane was estranged from her father, even until he died. She is estranged from her mother and never speaks to her siblings. She has volatile relationships with her children. She is divorced and now trying to make things work with a different man.

This is a tragic story, but having watched Jane throughout her life, I am certain that her pain and struggles are largely self-imposed through a lack of forgiveness. I've watched unforgiveness destroy her, and because of this, I am especially aware of the power of forgiveness and the way it can transform our children's lives—or destroy their lives when they refuse to walk in it. I also understand the struggles that people face with forgiveness, both in receiving it from God and in learning to extend it fully and effectively to others.

None of us want our children to become bitter and unforgiving people like Jane. And none of us want to become like her, either. Yet too many parents struggle with forgiving their kids—they get angry when their kids don't do what they should, and then that anger builds into bitterness and strife in the household. And a bitter, unforgiving spirit gets modeled for their children, and then the children become unforgiving as well. Therefore, learning to forgive readily and easily is critical for both—kids and parents.

God's unconditional forgiveness

(*Erin*)

Whether parents or children, at the very heart of our salvation is God's forgiveness. He forgives us our sin, not because He owes us anything or because we deserve it, but because He loves us. That's it. Roll that around in your brain for just a second. God forgives us our iniquity because He loves us and wants a relationship with us unhindered by our sin.

When I consider this, I am overcome with His incredible love—for me and for each of my children. He chose to forgive me simply because I asked and He loved me enough to do it. No hard feelings. No grudges. No regrets. Just pure, unconditional forgiveness.

What a gift! Every time we falter, every rude word, every misguided promise, every untrusting moment, every mistake we make is forgiven—without hesitation. And each time our child falters, is rude, or makes a mistake, she is forgiven as well.

Yet, before any of us can have a heart that is able to forgive, we first have to understand the rich and merciful gift of God's forgiveness. As parents, we must understand this, and then we must teach and model it to our children.

And, like His other characteristics, God's forgiveness is inherently complex. Therefore, I encourage you to spend time meditating and reading about God's forgiveness. It will speak to your heart and help you to understand not only how to forgive others, but it will also show you how to teach your children about forgiveness.

Here are a few of the things I learned from my own study:

- God is merciful to us, showering us with forgiveness when we confess our sins (Proverbs 28:13).
- God forgives ALL unrighteousness. There is no sin that can outlast God's forgiveness if we are willing to confess and repent (1 John 1:9).
- God gave of Himself in order that He could redeem our unrighteousness (Titus 2:14).

- God loves us even while we are sinners (Romans 5:8).
- God offers forgiveness out of His compassion for us, giving us freedom and hope (Isaiah 30:18).
- There is no further condemnation once we are forgiven. If we repent and ask for forgiveness, our slate is wiped clean (Romans 8:1).
- Once we are forgiven, our sins are removed from us as far as the east is from the west (Psalm 103:12).

Wouldn't it be wonderful if we could learn to forgive others as Christ forgives us? And wouldn't it be great if we could teach our children this important principle? Though our human emotions and human conflicts make it hard for us to handle things in a way that facilitates perfect forgiveness, the act of forgiving is often the key that sets our hearts free from the instability that comes from the burden of sin and the pain of our fallen world. And when our hearts can forgive, our kids can see how it works and be free to grow, learn, make mistakes, learn from them, and be sanctified in the process.

When a heart can't forgive

(Ellen)

Remember the story about my friend Jane who harbored unforgiveness in her heart for years? She obviously didn't learn how to forgive, and she chose to become bitter. Jane needed forgiveness modeled, taught, and imparted to her. But that didn't happen, and it destroyed her.

Don't let this be your child's story. I urge you to help your kids not only understand the forgiveness that they have been given in Christ, but also learn how they can give others the precious gift of forgiveness.

As I started studying forgiveness more in depth, I honestly got confused. Luke 6:37—probably the most quoted verse on forgiveness—says "Forgive, and you will be forgiven." This implies that our forgiveness from God is contingent upon our own ability to forgive. Yet, in other places of the Bible, God forgives people through His mercy. In Matthew 9:2, Jesus tells the crippled man to, "Get up! Your sins have been forgiven." Later, Jesus explains to the crowd that He has been given all authority to forgive our sins, out of the great and powerful mercy of the Father.

I had a difficult time reconciling these two verses. Is forgiveness a merciful gift, given to each of us as we confess and repent? Or is it contingent on our own ability to forgive others? It's both. Like salvation, God offers His forgiveness as a free and powerful gift. If we confess our sins and repent, He will forgive us and wash us clean as snow.

But, when we choose not to forgive others, it is a sin—a sin that can cause our heart to grow bitter. And only by confessing and repenting of the sin of unforgiveness can we experience the grace of God. I believe that people who harbor unforgiveness will struggle in their relationships both with people and with God. This isn't because they aren't saved—we are saved through faith by grace—but simply because they have unrepentant sin in their lives.

Do you ever see this happening in your own heart? And do you ever see this happening in the heart of your child? It's never too late to repent and to forgive like Jesus forgave you. He will wash you clean as snow—and your iniquities will be forgotten. Likewise, if your children are struggling with forgiveness, below are some strategies for teaching healthy conflict resolution skills, which can help children learn how to forgive.

Healthy conflict resolution that can lead to forgiveness

Probably one of the most disturbing behaviors that I observe in both children and adults is what I call "fight or flight conflict." It's an adrenaline-caused reflex that, when a human is faced with danger, he will impulsively either fight—i.e. pick up a stick and beat the rabid dog that's charging him—or run from the dog. This behavior may serve us well should we face wild animals, but as parents, it doesn't serve us well when it comes to conflict.

A few weeks ago, I was asked to counsel two high school girls. One of the girls, Sara, had inadvertently hurt her best friend, Amanda's, feelings. Amanda, a "fighter," responds to conflict with anger-based attitudes—and so she walked up to Sara and confronted her. Sara, a "flighter," listened to Amanda's verbal tirade and simply clammed up and walked away.

Both of these girls responded in a way that led to unforgiveness and more anger. As a result, their friendship disintegrated. Amanda was shocked that Sara didn't even respond to her complaint and stormed off with her anger simmering but silent. Sara was so upset that Amanda had yelled at her that she went home and sulked in her bedroom, crying for hours, but refusing to discuss her feelings. It was a no-win situation, and both girls suffered.

One of the most important things we can teach our kids is how to deal with conflict in a way that leads to restoration and forgiveness. Although this can be a hard thing for kids to learn, especially when emotions make situations volatile, giving them good, godly conflict resolution skills will serve our kids well. They need these skills, not only when faced with conflict with their friends, but also in their future working relationships and even their marriages.

Picture a triangle. The top point of the triangle represents God and his perfect forgiveness. He's slow to anger, yet even-handed. He's compassionate, yet honest. He's forgiving regardless of circumstances. He delivers justice, but also provides mercy. (Get a free downloadable copy of the one below at www.familywings.org.)

On the bottom left point of the triangle are flight-based responses to conflict—behaviors like running, avoiding, and sulking. And on the bottom right point of the triangle are fight-based responses to conflict like screaming, yelling, and lashing out. As you see, both responses are as far away from a Christ-like response to resolving conflict as you can get.

Each of us should work on bringing our responses closer to God's style of forgiveness. By intentionally adopting Christ-like responses—like careful and kind conversation, prayer and compassion—His attributes of mercy and love are shown to the other person, and our relationship grows. And while none of us can be perfect in our responses, we should strive to respond as close to God's perfect forgiveness as possible.

TOOLS THAT CAN LEAD TO FORGIVENESS

So, how do you help your kids develop a heart that is willing to forgive when true emotions like anger, frustration, and sadness are part of living life together? Here are some ideas:

Tool #1: A home where forgiveness resides

One of the best gifts we can give our kids is a home that is a place of rest and shelter. And in order to create that ambiance, your home must be a place where forgiveness resides. As parents, we must intentionally and purposefully model forgiveness personally, with our spouse, and with our children. That means asking for forgiveness when you need it and mercifully offering it when others need it.

Intentionally plant "forgiveness seeds" in your kids' hearts through prayer and Bible stories, and water them regularly both by extending forgiveness to them and by guiding them to forgive others. Otherwise, the "weeds of offense" will take root and sprout nasty self-focused responses that become harder and harder to get rid of. Your children will not naturally choose to forgive unconditionally. Rather their human nature, as well as the narcissistic culture they are surrounded by, will nurture the growth of selfish attitudes. Only by careful and intentional cultivation can forgiveness become a comfortable habit.

Tool # 2: Be a mentor

Have you ever caught yourself saying something like "don't fight," or "go work it out," to your kids? I sure have! And if I'm being honest, sometimes the best remedy to calming down siblings who are constantly bickering is to let them work it out themselves. But there are also times when parents should intentionally show your kids what effective conflict resolution looks like. The next time your kids get into an argument, sit down with them, and model good conflict resolution. Show them how to express their anger in an appropriate way, and then teach them how to respond with forgiveness and grace.

Tool #3: Don't live unoffended; live forgiven

I used to counsel people to "live unoffended"—to not let offenses affect them. But this counsel was incorrect and confusing, because, while it's important to let small infractions go, often leaving a conflict "unoffended" can lead to further offense and hurt. It's important to find the balance between being offended at every little thing and stuffing an offense until it festers and grows into bitterness.

So, while you should do your best to overlook minor issues without letting it become a conflict or offense, if a major issue comes up, don't refuse to address it just because you are trying to live "unoffended." Instead, be intentional about addressing valid conflicts and readily offer forgiveness so that offenses don't fester.

Tool # 4: Normalize conflict

Conflict needs to be normalized for our kids and not feared. When they come to see conflict as a normal part of human relationships, they will be less likely to run from it or be hurt by it. This paves the way for them to learn how to manage conflict and confrontation well.

Tool # 5: Read about God's forgiveness

It often goes against our human nature to forgive, which is why it's so hard for some of us to let go of an offense. Yet, the best way to foster a heart that forgives is through careful study of God's forgiveness. By spending time in the Word and carefully studying God's perfect forgiveness, we can gain an attitude of mercy and compassion. And the next time you feel angry, you'll be more equipped to respond like Jesus would.

Likewise, our kids need to see what God's forgiveness looks like. Spend time reading Scripture together, and talk about what forgiveness looks like. Then, discuss how and why we as humans struggle to forgive and ask your kids if they struggle to forgive. Then, come up with a plan to forgive God's way in the future.

A prayer for forgiveness

Father God, in Your great mercy, You have blessed me with inexplicable forgiveness. I am so blessed! Lord, give me a heart that forgives others so that I can feel the joy of Your forgiveness. Help me not to find offense in small things, and when I do feel offended, help me to deal with it in a way that leads to restoration and forgiveness. Amen.

Verses for further study

1 John 1:9
Isaiah 1:18
Jeremiah 31:3
Romans 5

Chapter 8

REPLACE GRUMBLING WITH GRATITUDE

(Ellen)

Our school has a special tradition we follow each year. The week before Thanksgiving, the kindergarteners perform a beautiful ritual. One by one they walk through a wrought iron gate that leads to a small garden on our campus. And as they enter through the gates, each one is asked to look toward heaven and proclaim at least one thing that they are thankful for.

The parents and teachers sit to the side and watch these precious little children express their gratitude to our Father in a way that's not only observable, but also meaningful. I love it! And this year, I loved it more than ever because two of my grandchildren are in kindergarten. I got quite a laugh when my grandson Jude walked through that gate and proclaimed his eternal gratitude for fresh air!

We certainly do have much to be thankful for! But more than that, I've learned that, although giving thanks is a simple gesture, it is fundamentally profound and deeply life changing. In fact, I believe heartfelt gratitude, or appreciation, is the basis of true pleasure. Have you noticed how joy-filled people are also very grateful people? A few years ago, I was blessed by reading *One Thousand Gifts* by Ann Voskamp. In her book, she dares us to live "fully" right where God has placed us, and she challenges us to understand that by choosing to be grateful, we are able to do just that.

It is God's will for us (1 Thessalonians 5:16-18) to rejoice, pray, and give thanks to Him in everything—not merely for what gives us joy, but also in every circumstance that we find ourselves in, no matter how challenging. God works powerfully in hearts that are inexplicably and undeniably grateful.

The apostle Paul tells us to "rejoice always." I'm not saying that we should celebrate when bad things do happen, but we are to never allow the mud of troublesome times to blind our vision of eternity. Because we serve a God who has overcome the world, we can take heart in times of trouble and choose to be grateful for His overcoming power.

What an amazing privilege and opportunity we have to enter His gates with thanksgiving and His courts with praise (Psalm 100:4)! It is a place where our enemy can't reach us, and God, in his loving compassion, takes over for us. His courts are where prayers are answered and miracles occur. It is where we find contentment and healing and peace. It is where we find rest, and where our worries and anxieties are defeated. It is where we find supernatural joy when we experience the very things we thought would overwhelm us.

This is what our kids need to see. Our children need parents who believe what God says—parents whose hearts are at peace and not overwhelmed by the circumstances of life. They need parents who choose to be grateful, not just for their blessings, but also in their frustrations, hurts, worries, anxieties, fear, and even in their disappointments and failures. These are the parents who model that they trust God to intercede in all of their lives.

And this is the kind of faith that will transform your family.

Gratitude simple—but hard

The act of giving thanks is simple—in its essence.

It involves simple words, simple thoughts, and simple unadorned acts of recognizing the incredible gifts that we have.

It's so innately simple, in fact, that gratitude is often overlooked as a spiritual discipline. People look to "disciplines" that seem more profound—prayer and fasting, the study of scripture and the act of forgiveness—as they search for spiritual meaning. But too often, we forget that simply showing gratitude can bring peace and light and hope to a troubled soul.

I want to encourage you to not complicate the act of gratitude. Instead, consider the power of this fundamentally simple act—to be grateful to a loving God for a beautiful world and for a blessed life. And leave it at that. Unadorned. Uncomplicated. But profoundly life-changing.

In everything give thanks

(*Erin*)

When I was pregnant, I was incredibly sick. I had morning sickness so badly that I was hospitalized multiple times, often for days, as doctors tried everything to help me eat. It was grueling—especially during my second and third pregnancies when I had other young children at home.

I remember during one hospital stay, a well-meaning woman from my church came to visit me, blessing me with flowers and chicken soup. As she left, she turned to me and said, "remember, in everything give thanks."

I burst into tears, feeling so inadequate to thank God for my illness, even if I was thankful for the pregnancy and the baby that was soon to come. And at that moment—in my emotionally fragile state—I understood that in order to be grateful, I had to be thankful *for* everything.

And if we're being honest, it's hard to be thankful for illness. Or death. Or destruction. Or poverty. Because those things are terrible—even if God is working in them and through them.

In 1 Thessalonians 5:18, when God asks us to be thankful in everything—He isn't asking us to pour out gratitude for tough circumstances. But instead, He wants us to pour out gratitude just because He is God, regardless of those tough circumstances. It's a small difference, but it's an important one.

So, be grateful that He is God. It's that simple. Be grateful that He sent His one and only Son to redeem us from a life of desperation and sin, and thank God He came to make us holy in His presence. No matter where you are circumstantially, no matter what you are doing, and no matter how your life is going, you have a wonderful gift every single day—and His name is Jesus.

And so, the next time your children fight with each other or your spouse lets you down; when your finances can't cover your bills or when your student presents a failing grade; when your toddler dismantles his room or breaks something precious to you; when your teen hurts your heart or when your project fails; when your friends slander you and when life is, well, life—be grateful! Not for the circumstance, but for the God who loves you fully, cares for you deeply, and is powerful and good and wonderful enough to bring you through it.

Pulling away from ungrateful attitudes

(*Ellen*)

When I am not abiding in a mindset of gratitude, I quickly begin to grumble and complain and focus on what's wrong. I think we all do it—just spend ten minutes listening to the conversations in a coffee shop, and I guarantee you'll hear a lot of pessimism.

It happens, and we fall into the trap. But living with an ungrateful heart is a miserable, shallow, and defeated way to live. Nobody can live fully, or purposefully, when they are focused on their problems.

For me, I know that the moment I start to grumble, my outlook changes, and I feel defeated and hard-pressed to make it through the day.

But if I turn my eyes toward Jesus and begin to thank Him for who He is and for what He gives, peace takes over. So does resolve and strength. And I begin to see my circumstances in a different light. I begin to understand that God looks for opportunities to intercede on my behalf. And those times I am feeling hopelessly discouraged and overwhelmed fade away into a peace that transcends understanding. Right in the midst of those dark, troubling times, as I choose to thank and trust Him with my circumstances, He responds to my offering of gratitude with the assurance and hope and steadfastness I need.

God loves me and desires to intercede on my behalf. He is our loving, faithful, all-knowing Father who wants us to run into His arms.

So, gratitude is our first line of defense against becoming overwhelmed and hopeless—and it is the path by which we can walk into His presence where His rest and His peace can take over. If you choose to replace grumbling with gratitude, not only will your perspective change, but you will also become a light of hope for your whole family.

TOOLS TO GUIDE A GRATEFUL HEART

Tool #1: Require please and thank you

I know it seems like a simple thing, but requiring your kids to say *please* and *thank you* can go a long way toward helping kids learn how to have a grateful heart. In fact, when I make sure to say *please* and *thank you*, my heart feels more grateful.

So I encourage you to make *please* and *thank you* a habit in your home by simply requiring your kids—and you as parents—to use these polite words whenever anyone asks for or receives something. If someone forgets, remind him or her, and then allow that person to try again. And before long, everyone will automatically be polite with their requests.

Tool #2: Replace grumbling with gratitude

It's easy to fall into the habit of grumbling—it certainly is for me when things seem to be going wrong. But a grumbling heart isn't a grateful heart, and so one of the easiest ways to teach kids to be grateful is to simply ask them to list things that they are thankful for whenever they start to whine or complain.

A few weeks ago, one of my grandchildren was grumbling about the food being served at our dinner table—a spread that her mother and I had spent more than an hour preparing. Instead of telling her "don't whine," or "eat it anyway"— which was my intuitive response—I asked her to start listing all the things on the table she was thankful for. At first it was just the milk, but as I encouraged her to keep on listing the positive, she added her siblings, the butter, the fruit—and the placemats. It was good start, and before long, there was a smile on her face, and she was happily munching on her least favorite parts of her dinner. Success!

Tool #3: Give thanks daily—and profusely

I encourage you to spend time each day thanking God for your blessings—for provision, family, homes, friends, food, and even for fresh air. The power of gratitude comes with the daily practice of gratitude, so spend time speaking and/or writing down your blessings and then recite them out loud to your kids.

One idea I love is to keep a thankfulness jar in your house. Have everyone jot down the things they are thankful for on slips of paper and drop them into the jar on a regular basis. Small children can even draw the things they are thankful for. Then, occasionally spend time reading through your notes, and rejoice together in the God from whom all blessings flow.

Tool #4: Intentionally focus on the good

To grumble and complain is a self-centered focus. No matter how real or true or right it feels, it's most often me-focused. And, oh, how easy it is to get caught up in grumbling and complaining, and then we justify that choice by pointing out "my right" to feel the way I do because things are "bad for me right now."

Every day we choose how we will view life's circumstances—to live by the lens of gratitude or to have our vision darkened by the lens of a complaining spirit. While nothing can separate us from God's love, complaining can certainly disrupt our intimate fellowship with Him, as well as our friendship with others. Choose gratitude!

Tool #5: Spend time with grateful people

Who doesn't love to be around people who inspire them and lift them up? A grateful person is willing to trust God and see the "silver lining." It buoys the heart to spend time with this kind of person.

Individuals with a grateful attitude are among the most mature people I know. Through purposeful choices and practice, thanksgiving wells up out of the core of who they are. They understand that to "rejoice always" and "to give thanks in everything" is not only a virtuous choice, but it is the will of God for each of us (1 Thessalonians 5).

Grateful people don't have fewer issues to contend with. They simply have discovered the supernatural joy and power that comes from experiencing difficulties, and then trusting and choosing a grateful mindset. They also constructively address concerns without grumbling about the circumstances—or others.

Gratitude is contagious, but so is grumbling, and it's an easy habit to fall into. For some, the habitual nature of grumbling has them continually finding something to be annoyed about. It's as if contentment is uncomfortable, and so they seek after something to grumble about. In a school community, or any community for that matter, this mindset causes more disunity and wastes more time than any other issue.

And I believe it spreads to children. They learn how to respond from the adults in their lives. Showing appreciation and being grateful is a simple, yet powerful way to speak life into others. Not only is it affirming, but it's also infectious.

Tool #6: Excel in generosity

It's better to give than to receive. Nothing fosters gratitude more than being generous with your time and treasure. So excel in being generous. The most grateful people I know are also the most generous. And happy. Therefore, give your kids regular opportunities to practice generosity and service both inside and outside of your home.

A prayer for gratitude

Father God, I am profoundly grateful for You. Without You, I would have no hope, no joy, and no purpose. But I do have hope, joy, and purpose, and so many other wonderful things because of You and the gift of Your Son. I choose to be thankful, and I am filled with gratitude! Lord, create in me an ever-grateful heart, one that is willing to give thanks in all situations. Help me to demonstrate gratitude for my kids so that they, too, will know the profound impact that a grateful spirit can have. Amen.

Verses for further study

1 Thessalonians 5:16-18
Psalm 100:1-5
Philippians 4:12-13
Ephesians 1:16-18
Matthew 6:21
Psalm 50:23

Chapter 9

REPLACE DISTRACTEDNESS WITH REST

(Ellen)

New Years Day, 2001. The new year signaled a new beginning, yet my heart ached knowing I was soon going to have an empty nest. And I had to figure out how to replace the fear of an empty nest with the faith I knew God wanted me to have.

It was an overwhelming milestone in my life: Glen and I would become empty nesters. Our youngest daughter, Alisa, was just finishing her senior year and would be heading to the University of Texas in the fall. My oldest daughter had just gotten married, and my son would start his senior year in college.

I woke early and found a quiet place downstairs that New Year's morning. It was cold, and snowflakes whispered softly to the ground outside our Oregon home. I poured water into the coffeepot and added freshly ground beans to the percolator. Then I went into the living room to add wood to the fire.

A few minutes later, I settled on the couch, a steaming mug of coffee in my hands, and I tore the wrapper off of the new journal I had purchased on a whim the day before. My New Year's resolution was to begin this new and different journey toward empty nesting with a daily, intentional dose of prayer, contemplation, journaling, and Scripture.

I contemplated my place in life. I had three great kids—each off doing great things and following the Lord while they did it. I had a loving husband, a good job, a great church. Yet, part of me was sad. Empty even. And perplexingly anxious.

My heart yearned for more.

I sat there that morning and allowed the profound soul sadness to surface—to reveal itself. I was tired of stuffing, of pretending all was well. As I sat in the quiet, a longing for something I could not put my finger on grew and grew. Looking back, I know God was pulling on my heartstrings. He wanted me to focus on Him—to turn my gaze away from all that had captured my attention for so many years. He was drawing me to begin to seek Him first, but I had no idea how to do that.

So, it was on that day, I began to write in my first journal—a daily habit that has continued to this day. I still remember what I wrote that morning: *"Lord, I want to know You—to see You more clearly."*

That was it.

A simple prayer.

Just one line.

It was all I had in me. It felt as if all those years of working so hard to get motherhood right had left me spiritually bankrupt. But God used that simple prayer to turn my spiritual life upside down. And since that morning, I haven't been the same. Slowly, but surely, my hunger to know God began to intensify as I took steps towards Him.

In the beginning of this journey, I was tentative—as if I was afraid of what I would discover as I sought Him. But I trudged on.

Some mornings, I read books about pursuing Him, which at first were rather incomprehensible to me. Other mornings, I dove into the Scripture with abandon. Still other days, I prayed, desperately, hopefully, intimately.

And, slowly, God used these times to move my soul, to transform me. My journal pages began to fill with prayers and personal revelations. Scripture came alive. And what started out as duty, turned into times that energized and refreshed my soul. Seeking Him first and purposely focusing on Him became essential manna for my heart.

Since then, God has continued to faithfully answer that prayer— "I want to know you more." Each time I begin to fall back into old habits—and sadly, at times I do—He mercifully intervenes. There have been many small interventions—and a few big ones—but each time, He has taught me that only by pressing into Him will I truly be fulfilled and free from the anxious thoughts that threaten to overwhelm me.

I want my kids to know this fulfillment.

And I want your kids to know it as well.

There is nothing in the human experience that can fill us, move us, satisfy us, or placate us like Jesus can.

Nothing.

And so, by learning to "attend to Him"—to stay in-tune with His voice in your life—you can learn to live a satisfied, peace-filled life, free from the fears that threaten to engulf you.

The habit of quiet time

Over the years, I've worked hard to develop a habit of daily quiet time, because I learned long ago that the key to finding solace and satisfaction in Christ is by spending time with Him. And, as I'm sure you've discovered, the more time you spend with Him, the more you will crave spending time with Him.

But finding the time and energy and desire for a daily quiet time can be a challenge, especially with our busy lives. And that's why I want to encourage you to be very intentional about developing this habit. I challenge you to make it a family affair and implore you to help your kids develop the habit early on.

Here are some tips:

1. **Discuss quiet time as a family and make a plan.** Quiet time is a personal thing—the point is that you do it in solitude. That said, if your family wants to develop the habit of daily quiet time, I think the

first step is to make a plan. Tell your kids that your family is starting to do "quiet time," explain what your expectations are for it, and then have each person make suggestions and comments as to how to make that time a success.

2. **Hold yourselves accountable.** Hold yourself and your kids accountable to implementing quiet time. If your kids are young, maybe a check-box chart or a sticker chart would work. If they are older, discuss what you are learning in quiet time as a family once a week at dinner.

3. **Set a time that works for you.** I do my quiet time first thing in the morning, before the sun rises. For me, this works, because I've always been an early riser, and I love starting my day with Jesus. But I'm not naïve enough to think that a five-in-the-morning quiet time would work for all people. So, if you're more focused at night, then by all means, do it at night. And that goes for your spouse and kids as well.

4. **Let your kids set a time that works for them.** Just as adults have times that they focus best, kids do, too. So don't pressure your kids to do their quiet time at the same time as you. Instead, encourage them to choose a regular time that's best for them, and give them the tools they need (a quiet room, a Bible, a journal) to be successful.

5. **Share your journey.** Make sure you are sharing your quiet-time journey openly and honestly with your kids so that they, too, will learn how to reflect on and then share their personal spiritual journey with you.

Learning to be still

For many years, I've been working to develop stillness as a consistent discipline in my life, and while I have certainly improved, I have a long way to go. To be still, in our culture, is almost an oxymoron. Many of us seek solitude and stillness, but with our busy lives and mile-long to-do lists, stillness often gets pushed aside. And even when we do find the time to be still, our minds race with a flurry of thoughts that are anything but still.

Being still isn't about physical stillness. Rather, it is about being free from an *internal state* of agitation or excitement. Because of the distracted world we live in and the activity-driven nature of our society, practicing the discipline of "stillness"—or rest—is even more essential.

Yet, at those times when I most need to "be still," my human nature is often tempted to flip to "Ellen's gear." Then my thinking goes into adrenalin overdrive, and then I talk faster and work faster, growing more agitated but less fruitful. During those times, being an action-oriented person with a full agenda, my driven work ethic becomes my downfall.

I am learning, however, to recognize this pattern, and then I intentionally "flip the switch" by reminding myself who is ultimately in control. Thankfully, rest in God is never really out of reach, regardless of the circumstances. *God already knows what I need, and He is just waiting for me to calm down and rest enough to hear Him.*

I need to abide in this internal stillness when my workload is the heaviest and there is no end in sight. I need to abide there, in His quiet presence, in order to remain patient with my active (but very delightful) grandchildren. I need this discipline in order to walk wisely with students as they practice and learn to live out their faith.

Stillness restores peace to my heart amid dissension and equips me to respond lovingly to others rather than react impulsively. I need stillness when I am healthy or sick, weak or strong, pleased or displeased, confused or certain.

Stillness grounds me in the rest of God. Here I can be attentive to Him and hear His voice. And, in the stillness of His presence, the enemy leaves me alone.

What distracts us?

What distracts you from being still before God?

Is it busyness—the fact that you have a to-do list a mile long and only a limited amount of time to do it? Is it your job and your quest to do well in your career? Is it a perfect home? Is it entertainment like TV or books or iPad games? Or is it Facebook or Twitter—or my personal favorite, Pinterest?

We live in a world full of distractions. To illustrate this point, I want you to put this book down and relax, wherever you are, right now. Now, set a timer for five minutes, and in your mind, pay attention to every distraction that comes your way.

If your kids get into a squabble and scream for you, that's a distraction. If you see your iPad sitting next to you and get a sudden urge to check Facebook, that's a distraction. The pile of unfolded laundry sitting on your dresser. A distraction. And if your iPhone is taunting you to check your work email really quick, well, that is...you guessed it...a distraction.

How many distractions did you count in just five minutes? I counted ten, and I was trying my best to avoid them. That's the world we live in, and that makes me worry about my kids, your kids, and the future of our world.

We are surrounded by so many distractions, especially when it comes to media and technology. And that includes our kids. Each day I hear of some new social media form by which we can "connect" to others. It's impossible to keep up with all the new and distracting things that come our way. If this is our new reality, how then can we guide our children to not only use digital technology beneficially, but also to avoid the inherent pitfalls that come with it?

We are raising kids in a culture like none we've experienced before—one in which they can carry with them information about any topic, both good and bad, and have the ability to connect to anyone, anywhere, at any time. No other generation has had, at their fingertips, the incredible opportunities that today's digital world grants—nor the menacing snare that it can easily become. Adults, teens, and even toddlers are easily mesmerized by these tools. And although they are intended to improve our lives, they can also become our downfall.

At this moment, you can find any number of articles about how technology can enhance a child's development. You can also find an equal number of articles about how it harms the process. It's the same with social media. Every day I come across new articles and recommended books that discuss the impact of digital technology on our children.

The bottom line? Parents *must* be wise.

But how do we even begin?

My advice? Begin by keeping the end in mind.

When they are grown, what do we want from our kids? What do we want them to be like? What might today's young children, many of whom are being raised on a heavy digital diet, grow up to be like? And what can we do to counteract the downside of their digital exposure so that they will not wind up with short attention spans, negative memory issues, trouble with interpersonal relationships, and difficulty in understanding true emotions?

Though our kids live in a distracted world, that doesn't mean they must live distracted lives. Instead, if we point them daily toward the reality that they are loved and valued and that they matter deeply to a holy God, and if we show them how to tune their hearts to God, they will learn how to attend to and prioritize the things that really matter. The truth is, He alone can fill the void in their hearts—that yearning for connectedness, for meaning, and for everlasting love.

As parents, in order to help them learn this balance, we need to be serious about setting limits and firm guidelines regarding how our kids use technology and media. It's essential for any family. I encourage you to read up on what that looks like, and I recommend *The Digital Invasion* by Dr. Archibald Hart and Dr. Sylvia Hart Frejd. In this book, one of the key components to successfully teaching your kids how avoid being distracted and consumed by technology is not by taking away the distractions, but instead by teaching them how to attend to what really matters—essentially, to stay in-tune with His voice.

Today's kids need to learn how to use technology wisely, yet still gain vital disciplines of the heart and mind that are nurtured outside the digital world. And as a parent, the first step you can take towards finding this balance is teaching your child to have a heart that is able to attend to God and his quiet voice—a voice that is often only heard when someone is willing to take the time to be still and pay attention.

Internal distractions

It's pretty easy to pinpoint what distract us in our world. But internal distractions—those spiritual habits, struggles and sins that draw us away from abiding in Jesus—are another story.

For me, the internal distraction that affects me most is my innate desire to please people. I can easily get overly consumed with attending to the needs and demands of others. I then, without meaning to, start to substitute doing good things for authentically seeking after the One who is good. And I know I am allowing myself to be distracted by my pleasing nature when a familiar weariness of soul begins to set in. It's the result of a focus that is turned toward things below rather than on things above.

Slowly, over the years, I am learning—and relearning—that the trials of life, the demands of others, and the circumstances I find myself in must not become my primary focus. Rather, in the midst of these, I must attend to God, and He will keep me steadfast and provide a way through whatever I face in life—in an abundantly rich and meaningful way.

A primary internal distraction I see, particularly among adolescents and young adults, is the propensity to find things to grumble and complain about. It's a contagious mindset, a distraction spurred on by social media, that not only distorts reality but also distracts from all that God has in mind for us. The antidote is to focus instead on being grateful and content.

TOOLS TO ENCOURAGE A FOCUS ON HIM

I still think back to that January morning in 2001. In some ways, I had begun to think that without my role as a mom, I would no longer be fulfilled. But in God's great mercy, I found it was just the opposite. God used that time to refocus my soul on Him and bring me deeper satisfaction than I had ever had before. While each person needs to take that same spiritual journey, as parents, we can teach our kids how to start pursuing God.

Tool #1: Model attention to God

Show your kids what it looks like to attend to God. Put your cell phone and laptop away, and go somewhere quiet. My friend, Kathy, always does her quiet time on her covered back patio—rain or shine or snow. She says she's found that, if she tries to focus on God in her house, she's constantly distracted. So she's made sure to find a place where she can focus on God. Her kids now know that if she's outside with her Bible on the patio, they can't distract her, short of a major emergency. When it's cold, she just bundles up and wraps herself in a warm blanket. Whatever you decide is best for you, let your children see how important your time with God is to you.

Tool #2: Try journaling

My daughter, Erin, takes after me in that she loves to use a prayer journal to write down her prayers and conversations with God. When my grandson, Joey, was four, Erin gave him a prayer journal so that he, too, could record his conversations with God. At first, it was just squiggling lines and pictures, but he began to develop the habit. Now he can read and write, and he often writes full prayers, or he sketches his thoughts and feelings. I love that he's taken to journaling at such an early age.

Tool #3: Memorize scripture as a family

It's essential that we store up God's Word in our hearts so that we can attend to His truths at any time. I think one of the best ways to do this is to memorize Scripture as a family, and you can start your kids at an early age. Choose a verse, each month or week, to memorize as a family. Or let your kids choose their favorite sections and then recite them to you as they learn them. Filling your home—and your minds—with God's Word will bolster your faith like little else can.

Tool #4: Keep a NOT to do list

Our natural inclination is to attend to things that require little thought. This is especially true of adolescents who are so very interested in the social aspects of their lives. They likely know what their "to do" list should look like but knowing what should be on their "NOT to do" list at a given time may be even more important. This list should include those distractions that require little thought and thus are so tempting. It's why I have learned to keep my cell phone out of my quiet times so that my mind is not tempted to be pulled away from what is most life giving, and satisfying, to my soul.

A prayer for faith

Father God, I know that my soul will never be truly satisfied or at peace if it's not in tune with You. Help me to eliminate the distractions of this world and within myself so that I can seek You. Help me to be a model for my kids as they learn to attend to Your voice. Give them hearts that seek You and minds that want to know You better. Amen.

Verses for further study

Isaiah 30:15
Mark 4:24
Proverbs 5:1
Proverbs 2:1-5
Proverbs 1:7
Exodus 15:26
Matthew 13:15
Zechariah 7

Chapter 10
REPLACE HOPELESSNESS WITH HOPE

(Erin)

Parenthood is a journey, but it isn't always beautiful.

Instead, it often twists down a path with many ups and downs. The journey of parenting has some of the highest peaks—places where the sunrise will nearly take your breath away, days full of color and light, and lots of sticky-fingered hugs.

I can't help but get teary when I think of those beautiful moments—the exuberant high-five I got after my son Joey first learned to ride his bike. The toothless smile from Kate when she finished her kindergarten "Thankfulness" presentation. Watching my husband hoist my son Will on his shoulders to help him shoot a basket he couldn't quite reach.

But there are also low and dark places, those days when parenthood yanks us through difficult tangles and brambles and takes us deep into the heart of our darkest places. Places where darkness closes in, where God seemed all-too distant, and where we simply don't have the strength to take another step forward.

Places where hope seems lost.

These are times like when my sister, Alisa, sat heartbroken in the front seat of a little red car in a hospital parking lot because, in the back seat, a pink-ruffled infant car seat sat empty. Or another time, on the cold bathroom floor on a rainy Tuesday night when I huddled down and cried for a baby that would never take a single breath. And even the time in a lonely NICU when our entire family watched as my tiny nephew Asa struggled for his next breath even before he had a name to call his own.

Have you ever been in such a place? That place of hopelessness? That place of loss? That cold and lonely rock-bottom place in the parenting journey when darkness rules and hope seems futile? Fighting for breath, grasping at sanity, hearing echoes of your childhood anthems that tell you to "pull yourself up by your bootstraps"? And you hope, wide-eyed, for a second, that you are strong enough to pull through.

You aren't.

In a very real sense, a mother's (and a father's) heart is birthed on the day their first child is born. It is also laid bare to receive the greatest outpouring of love and joy and hope that you could ever imagine. But it is also laid hopelessly vulnerable to be stomped on, spit on, wounded, and betrayed. With every success and failure, every pain and joy, the parent's heart beats right alongside the heartbeat of the child.

The parenting journey is excruciatingly beautiful and excruciatingly painful—sometimes at the same time. And with such a depth of emotion, it's easy to get lost in a wave of hopelessness, to get stuck in the muck of everyday life, and to forget the true promise of hope that He has for us.

There is a hope that goes beyond human understanding, a hope that climbs above all the ups and downs of everyday life and a hope that lets us walk in His light, even when we are trudging through the depths of despair. But we can't find that light on our own. And often, the harder we try to parent in our own strength, the more desperate we are to cling to our kid's grimy hands and yank them out of the muck, the more lost we feel. The truth is, no one is really strong enough to meet all the challenges of the ups and downs of parenting.

Except Him.

God is enough.

God is strong enough.

That's the anthem that should echo through our minds as we parent, allowing hope to trickle in and life and grace to overcome the pain of this world. We cannot parent well by our own volition or in our own strength, but we can through *His* strength.

We are fully aware that simple words like "God is enough" can sound just as trite and useless as words like "pull yourself up by your bootstraps." There is no magic pill to bring hope when you hit rock bottom and slide into those dark places. And even when you allow God to shoulder the brunt of your parenting journey, you will probably still cry many tears. But imagine how painful it would be without God? Without the only One who is strong enough?

My parenting journey is messy, beautiful, frantic, triumphant, and, at times, tragic. But it is real. And with time, I've come to see the hope that comes by simply putting my trust in Him and allowing God's tender embrace to pull me out of my pit and into a place of strength.

I trust that God is writing a beautiful and strong story with your life and in your family. But how can you put that hope in Him?

The hope that comes from Him

(Ellen)

It's been more than thirty-five years since I first held Erin in my arms, yet I can still close my eyes and feel the warmth of her tiny body nestled against me. I can still picture her wearing a tiny yellow-and-white bonnet that I had carefully sewn during my pregnancy—in neutral colors just in case my mother's intuition was wrong. I can still take a deep breath and smell that baby-powder-meets-softness smell that seemed to surround her in those days. Even now, if I close my eyes and picture my precious newborn daughter, my heart starts to race with the incredible joy and hope that came with those first days of her life.

There is no way to describe those feelings but to say that my heart beat *for* her. You know what I mean, don't you? It was as if, instantly, my life's dreams and hopes and desires had a new focus, my life had a new purpose, and I would've done anything for my daughter.

Anything.

So I began to dream about her future. What kind of personality would she have? Would she be competitive or easy going? Extroverted or introverted? Would she seek Jesus and follow Him in whatever unique calling He might have for her, or would she ultimately choose to deny Him?

My hopes and dreams for her continued to grow as Erin grew. I remember one cold, winter night when Erin was eleven or twelve. Glen and I pondered what would become of Erin. My heart hurt for her, and like so many parents of adolescents, we were anxious—and nearing hopelessness—over the direction our daughter was heading.

Erin had great ideas, but she was too disorganized to carry them out. She had strong interests, but she was not very self-directed. Erin could be caring and compassionate one minute, but then she would become hostile the next. She was volatile and impulsive. Erin would no longer merely accept what we had to say, but, instead, she vehemently fought us at every turn. She wanted to do things her way, even if the results were disastrous.

As parents, we were quickly falling into a deep, dark place of hopelessness as we watched our daughter's downward spiral. So, I understand the feelings of hopelessness that a parent can experience, especially in the adolescents years, as a child demands space to beat his own drum. The questions. The debates. The doubts and fears. They rock not only the child, but they also yank at the very heart of the parent.

As my husband and I fretted about Erin, we saw high school looming just around the corner, and we were terrified at what might happen to her! Gone was the secure feeling of parenting a young child—a child who once believed her parents held great wisdom. Now, she was a child who thought she possessed the wisdom to manage life on her own, even though we knew she didn't yet have what it would take to navigate those rough waters of adolescence.

So there we sat, with our eldest child in between childhood and adulthood, and we were scared of what the future held for her. That night, we talked and struggled to find any kind of solid ground with our daughter—to find the answers to what to do, to find the magic solution.

But those answers never came. God—in His great wisdom—didn't give us answers to parenting. He gave us the heart of a parent. Yes, we simply must parent with our hearts—and parent *to* our children's hearts—instead of parenting merely with our minds.

That is the key to hope, to our kid's futures—to everything. It's how we transfer faith from one generation to the next. Heart to heart.

The Bible has much to say about the heart, making it clear that the "heart" is not only aligned with the mind and the will, it is also closely associated with our feelings and affections. Joy begins in the heart. So does discouragement (Isaiah 65:14). Both love and hate reside there (1 Timothy 1:5, Leviticus 19:17). And the heart can be "deceitful above all things and desperately wicked" (Jeremiah 17:9). At the same time, the heart is the dwelling place of our God (Ephesians 3:17). It is the place where God does His most profound work. The "issues of life" flow from our hearts (Proverbs 4:23).

After more than thirty years of struggle, it's now clear that, as the "anointed disciplers of our children," we parents must first turn our hearts to God for our hope. We must spend our time on our knees, pleading for our children, as He reveals to us His plans for them, and who He is crafting them to become. And after we hear His voice and know what He wants, we must use the tools we have been given to speak truth and love to their hearts. Then, we will find the hope instead of the hopelessness that once existed. Then we will be truly free to parent!

In Psalm 127:1, we read that "unless the LORD builds the house (meaning household or family) those who build it labor in vain."

We cannot "build" our children. We cannot make them into who we want them to be. We can be used by God to hammer and chisel their character, but He is the Master Builder, the Sculptor.

Parents often take on hopelessness and pressure when they assume ownership of their children—ownership that rightly belongs to God. Yet, when we choose to let go of the weight of this burden and trust God with our children, the load becomes bearable, and hope is restored. We can then take on our rightful roles. And we can rest assured that the end result is in the hands of the Creator, the One who blessed us with unique children as a heritage, and the One who will walk with them throughout all their lives.

God blesses us with children who are indeed a gift and a heritage from Him (Psalm 127:3). They are to be treasured and cared for and delighted in, not only for the good that they accomplish but also when they mess up. They are to be loved for who they are, and their souls are to be tended to throughout the process of growing up.

No child is a mistake.

Each child is created intentionally with God's ultimate end in mind—to come to a saving faith in Jesus and to walk confidently in His calling for him or her, equipped to then transfer faith forward to the next generation.

That's what families are all about.

And it's where our hope lies.

A hope and a future

Where do you see your child in ten years? Close your eyes, and picture him or her. Picture her as a graduating senior. Picture him stepping onto a college campus or into his first job. Picture her getting married, and maybe having kids of her own.

What is the picture like?

I'm guessing you've pictured success—a graduation cap with the tassel hanging over his eyes; a diploma in her hand with bright job opportunities in her future; him marrying a beautiful bride; her looking picture-perfect with her beautiful family.

It's a nice picture, isn't it?

I don't think any parent would want anything less for her kids.

Nice. But it's not enough.

As Christians, we know there is much more to life than a diploma and a good job. And we also know that picture-perfect success is often far from picture perfect. And so, as we dream for our kids and work toward helping them fulfill their potential, we must dream for *more*.

Close your eyes again.

This time, instead of picturing your child "on the outside," try to picture him or her on the inside in ten years. What will her heart be like? Will he courageously lead his family closer to God? Will she be strong and virtuous, a woman that will truly be called blessed? Will he love God wholeheartedly and unwaveringly? Will he be leading his own kids to follow Him? These are the important questions, the dreams to dream, the hope for their futures.

As parents, teaching our kids to serve, love, and seek Jesus above all else should be our ultimate vision. Our goals need to be centered on this aim because this is true success.

The truth is, there is no cure-all solution to get to these goals. There is no magic pill that will help us to raise kids who love Jesus. There is no formulaic "one way." But there are tools for parents, and I hope this book is one of those tools. Not *the* tool. Not *the* answer. But *a* tool, *an* answer—a hand to hold as you navigate the tricky world of parenting your child's heart.

Our hope is that you can avoid common parenting traps and liberate your son's and daughter's spirits by:

- replacing reliance on you with full reliance on Him
- teaching the simplicity of the Gospel by which virtuous desires form and sincere obedience follows
- responding to them less in a punitive manner and more in a discipleship fashion
- being motivated primarily to connect with them rather than control them

- avoiding the trap of complacency by establishing a lifelong desire to grow
- teaching your kids and modeling for them God's deep love
- purposing to see that forgiveness flows in all directions so that anger does not prevail
- finding joy even in the darkest of hours by way of a grateful heart
- finding rest for your soul by maintaining eyes that see Jesus
- placing your hope in His promises for you and your children

The end goal

Each year in May, another group of young men and women walk across the stage at Veritas Academy and receive their diplomas. I always bring a box of Kleenex because graduation is very emotional for me. These students are not my own children, but I have walked along side many of their families—for years. I know the struggles some have had to work through, and I know the times of hopelessness that their parents have felt.

Each graduate has their own unique story, one that includes both the development of their individual strengths as well as overcoming personal weaknesses. Each has experienced both successes and failures, making wise choices as well as mistakes, having good times and bad times. I see how God has worked in it all to prepare them for their calling, and I see how He has used their weaknesses to develop resilience, compassion, and understanding. Even in their personal struggles, God has had a purpose in mind!

I think of Steven whose mom refused to accept a bleak diagnosis when he was young, regarding his social, mental, and emotional development. Instead she embarked on a difficult journey to help her son overcome his weaknesses. God had touched her heart and painted a different vision for her son—a vision above and beyond what the world had spoken—His vision.

I think of the many times she sat in my office and cried when it all seemed so hopeless. There were times when the staff concluded that it was unwise to keep him in a school where he struggled to succeed and to fit in. Still, as a mother with a vision for more, she persisted and battled for her son, persuading us to keep working with him. She held tight to her high hopes and dreams for her son, but she deeply worried if any of them would ever come to fruition. Sometimes she would become discouraged when he acted out in class or disobeyed at recess—which happened often in earlier years—or when he struggled to turn in his work throughout middle school, or when he found excuse after excuse for his social miscues.

But God had sparked a passion in this mother—to fight for the vision she held for him. And slowly, ever so slowly, that vision became reality. He began to improve and change and grow into the man God created him to be.

I remember talking to this mom, and we both grinned as we realized that we were no longer addressing the typical issues we had dealt with for so many years. No longer was he struggling in class. No longer was he struggling to make friends. And no longer was I seeing him in my office for behavioral concerns. In fact, he was thriving!

This boy's journey has included many painful stretches, but when he crossed that stage on graduation day, I silently cried, "well done." He is embarking on a path at a great university towards a major which none of us considered possible just a few years ago. But all this pales in comparison to the man he has become. Stephen has a resilient spirit, and he has developed strong character and is rooted in his faith. I look forward to seeing what his future holds.

I also think of Cynthia who, for years, was sullen, defiant, and disinterested in learning. When she was in eighth grade, her defiance escalated—fighting with her parents, arguing with peers and teachers. She grew withdrawn and disengaged, and she wanted nothing to do with a school that was faith-based. She wanted out!

But one day, in a student-led Bible study on campus, God opened up the eyes of her heart, and she began to see with spiritual eyes. Right before our eyes, Cynthia changed. A smile replaced her frown. Her educational disengagement was replaced by a passionate desire to learn.

In her case, the change was sudden and dramatic.

Cynthia graduated as a confident, joyful, young woman who, throughout her high school career, exhibited a deep desire to learn and a commitment to follow Christ. She took with her a stellar transcript with offers to continue her education at many prestigious schools.

While Steven's and Cynthia's stories are very different, they are also similar. Both struggled through tough times—times that rocked their parents' worlds, challenged their parents' hearts, and caused us all to question God's purpose for their lives. Yet, God's intervention in each of their lives is clear. I pray their true stories will give hope to you as you struggle with the imperfections in your own children.

Never give up hope in the vision that God has entrusted to you regarding your children. Even their imperfections and in all the resulting struggles, God will use it all to perfect them and make them into the people He plans for them to be.

The following poem was written by my friend, Jef Fowler, who serves as the Head of School at Veritas Academy in Austin, Texas. This is the school where I have had the privilege of working at for many years now, and it is the school where my grandchildren attend. This school strives to graduate students who are not only academically and socially successful, but also works hard to educate children who sincerely love Jesus.

Every year, one senior is chosen to win the "Veritas Valiant" award for his or her embodiment of Christ-like characteristics. This award expresses everything we want for our own children and for the students we love.

We believe this list can give you a vision during your parenting journey, a way to look above and beyond the day-to-day challenges of raising your children. We even encourage you to print it out (go to www.familywings.org) and hang it on your fridge.

This vision embodies the promise and the hope that we have from God for our children.

The Veritas Valiant

He or She is ...
the good man or woman speaking well;
the courageous defender who rises above his fear
to uphold Truth and protect the vulnerable;
the selfless, servant-leader—prepared, assured and poised;
the tenacious competitor—gracious in victory, resilient in defeat;
the contagiously joyful, hopeful, positive encourager of others;
the loyal, honorable, reliable man of constant character;
the attentive observer and industrious doer,
propelled by his own initiative;
the passionately purposeful, ambitious, adventurous spirit—
fully alive & engaged;
the wise, well-read, life-long learner—
ordered in reason and desires, delighting in wonder;
the compassionate, kind and generous helper of the hurting;
the irrepressible visionary—
informed of the past, mindful of the future,
master of the moment in pursuit of his calling;
the patient, sincere listener—
discerner of the heart and intents of others;
the witty, inquisitive, contemplative soul,
appreciative of silence & solitude;
the lover of all that is good, true and beautiful,
drinking deeply of it;
the champion of justice, but abounding in grace and mercy;
the humble, thankful, grateful child of God;
and the winsome witness of Christ, in word and in deed—
a man after God's own heart, a friend of the Almighty.

We pray that we have provided some insight, some direction, and most importantly, some hope. We also hope this can become your vision statement for your parenting—a list of characteristics, rather than a list of rules, that embody a vision of hope for you as you parent your precious children.

Dear friends,

We are so grateful to you, our readers, for taking the time to connect with our stories and our hearts in this book. We pray that through this book and the plethora of other amazing resources available to Christian parents, you will be able to find joy in your parenting and in your precious children.

We'd love to hear from you! Please feel free to connect with us via our websites, Ellen's at www.familywings.org and Erin's at www. christianmamasguide.com. We both blog regularly and love hearing from our readers.

Additionally, many free resources including the charts and lists mentioned in this book are available for free download on both of our blogs. So please drop by and let us know if you can't find anything. We are also working on a study guide to accompany this book as well as several other projects so make sure to sign up for our newsletters and be the first to know as new books release.

Best Wishes!

Ellen Schuknecht
And
Erin MacPherson

About Ellen Schuknecht

Ellen Schuknecht has been working as an educator for more than 35 years, with experience ranging from early childhood education, to high school advising, to family ministries counseling. Her heart is to minister to young families in a way that's real, doable and helps them find true joy in their life stage.

She has been married to Glen for almost 40 years and lives nearby her three grown children and her ten grandchildren. She blogs at www.familywings.org

About Erin MacPherson

Erin MacPherson is a busy mom of three who wants to come beside her readers not only as a confidante and Christian sister, but also as a friend who understands what it's like to juggle kids, life and a much-too-messy house. She has written five books, including The Christian Mama's Guide series (Harper Collins, 2013), and contributed to many more. Additionally, her work can be seen in a large variety of publications including Daily Guideposts, Nickelodeon, WeAreTeachers, Thriving Family Magazine, MomSense Magazine and more. She blogs at www.christianmamasguide.com.

Other Books by These Authors

Books by Erin MacPherson:

The Christian Mama's Guide to Having a Baby (Erin MacPherson, Harper Collins, 2013)

The Christian Mama's Guide to Baby's First Year (Erin MacPherson, Harper Collins, 2013)

The Christian Mama's Guide to Parenting a Toddler (Erin MacPherson, Harper Collins, 2013)

The Christian Mama's Guide to the First School Years (Erin MacPherson, Harper Collins, 2013)

Books Erin and/or Ellen have contributed to:

Praying God's Word for Your Life (Kathi Lipp, Revell, 2013)

Praying God's Word for Your Husband (Kathi Lipp, Revell, 2012)

I Need Some Help Here! Prayers for When Your Kids Don't Go According to Plan (Kathi Lipp, Revell, 2014)

Daily Guideposts for New Moms (2011)

21 Ways to Connect With Your Kids (Kathi Lipp, Harvest House, 2012)

Daily Guideposts 2012, 2013, 2014, 2015 and 2016

Coming Soon:

Free to Parent Workbook (Family Wings, LLC)

Made in the USA
Lexington, KY
02 September 2015